POETICA 27

SAPPHO
THROUGH ENGLISH POETRY

Poetica is a series of texts, translations and
miscellaneous works relating to poetry

SAPPHO

THROUGH ENGLISH POETRY

Edited and introduced by
Peter Jay & Caroline Lewis

ANVIL PRESS POETRY

Published in 1996
by Anvil Press Poetry Ltd
Neptune House 70 Royal Hill London SE10 8RF
www.anvilpresspoetry.com

Reprinted in 2001

Selection and Introduction
copyright © Peter Jay & Caroline Lewis 1996

This book is published with financial assistance from
The Arts Council of England

ISBN 0 85646 273 X

Designed and set in Monotype Plantin Light
and Monotype Times Greek SF by Anvil
Printed at Alden Press Limited
Oxford and Northampton

Contents

1   VERSIONS

2   REPRESENTATIONS

ACKNOWLEDGEMENTS

We are grateful to authors, publishers and their representatives for permission to reproduce copyright material in this anthology as follows:

RICHARD ALDINGTON: 'To Atthis' from *Des Imagistes* (1914), copyright the estate of Richard Aldington; ROBERT BAGG: for 'Sappho' from *The Scrawny Sonnets and Other Narratives*, copyright 1973 by the Board of Trustees of the University of Illinois, used with the permission of the University of Illinois Press; MARY BARNARD: from *Sappho: A New Translation* (1958) to University of California Press, copyright © 1958 The Regents of the University of California, © renewed 1984 Mary Barnard; OLGA BROUMAS and JANE MILLER: for the poem from *Black Holes, Black Stockings* (1985) to Wesleyan University Press; DAVID CONSTANTINE: for poems from *Watching for Dolphins* (1983) to Bloodaxe Books; GUY DAVENPORT: for poems from *7 Greeks* (1995), copyright © 1995 by Guy Davenport, used by permission of New Directions Publishing Corporation; THOMAS HARDY: 'Sapphic Fragment' from *The Complete Poems* (1981) by Thomas Hardy, reprinted by permission of Papermac, Macmillan; JOHN HOLLANDER: for 'After an Old Text' from *Spectral Emanations* (1978) to the author; A. E. HOUSMAN: from *The Collected Poems of A. E. Housman*, reprinted by permission of The Society of Authors as the literary representative of the Estate of A. E. Housman; in the USA © copyright 1922, © 1965 by Holt, Rinehart & Winston, copyright 1950 by Barclays Bank, Ltd. Reprinted by permission of Henry Holt & Co., Inc.; CAROLYN KIZER: excerpt from 'For Sappho / After Sappho' copyright © 1984 by Carolyn Kizer. Reprinted from *Yin* by Carolyn Kizer, with the permission of BOA Editions, Ltd., 92 Park Ave., Brockport, NY 14604; RICHMOND LATTIMORE: for the poems from *Greek Lyrics*, 2nd edition (1960) to the University of Chicago Press, copyright 1949, 1955 and 1960 by Richmond Lattimore; MICHAEL LONGLEY: for 'The Evening Star' to the author; ROBERT LOWELL: for part I of 'Three Letters to Anaktoria' from *Imitations* (1962) to Faber and Faber Ltd and Farrar, Straus and Giroux; EDNA ST VINCENT MILLAY: for the poem from *Collected Poems* (1956) to Harper & Row, Inc.; HONOR MOORE: for 'Cleis', copyright Honor Moore, 1984; from *Memoir* (1988), Chicory Blue Press, by permission of Honor Moore; EZRA POUND: for the poem from *Lustra* (1915), copyright 1926 by Ezra Pound, used by permission of New Directions Publishing Corporation and Faber and Faber Ltd; EDWIN ARLINGTON ROBINSON: for 'Doricha', reprinted with the permission of Simon and Schuster from *Collected Poems of Edwin Arlington Robinson* (New York: Macmillan, 1937); ALLEN TATE: for 'Farewell to Anactoria' from *Collected Poems 1919–1976* (1977) to Farrar, Straus and Giroux; SARA TEASDALE: for 'To Cleis' and part I of 'Sappho', reprinted with the permission of Simon and Schuster from *Collected Poems of Sara Teasdale* (New York: Macmillan, 1937); PETER WHIGHAM: for poems from *Things Common, Properly* (1984) to Anvil Press Poetry; WILLIAM CARLOS WILLIAMS: for the excerpt from *Paterson*, Book V, copyright © 1958 by William Carlos Williams. Used by permission of New Directions Publishing Corporation and Carcanet Press Ltd; DOUGLAS YOUNG: for poems from *Auntran Ballads* (1943) to William McLellan.

We have made every effort to trace copyright holders, but if we have failed in any cases we would be glad to hear from those concerned.

Introduction

> Some say there were nine Muses. Count again.
> Look at Sappho of Lesbos: she makes ten.
>
> – PLATO

SAPPHO, CATULLUS, VILLON: these three poets were the touch-stones by which Ezra Pound believed lyric poetry should be judged, and their example was at the heart of the principles of Imagism. Apart from their intrinsic interest as poets, they are critical for the modern movement as a whole; and equally so for poetry today.

'The Imagistes admitted', wrote F.S. Flint in 1913, 'that they were contemporaries of the Post-Impressionists and the Futurists; but they had nothing in common with these schools. They had not published a manifesto. They were not a revolutionary school; their only endeavour was to write in accordance with the best tradition, as they found it in the best writers of all time – in Sappho, Catullus, Villon.' And Pound: 'If you want the gist of the matter go to Sappho, Catullus, Villon, Heine when he is in the vein, Gautier when he is not too frigid…'

The main purpose of this book is to sketch how Sappho has fared in English: what poets and translators have made of her poems through the centuries, and what they have made of her, or perhaps one should say 'her', that is, her image. For the truth is that we know almost nothing about the historical Sappho, but a great deal (too much, one might say) about what she has become at various points for other people.

It is widely assumed that Sappho's poems and fragments are auto-biographical. There is no way either to prove or disprove this assumption, which is not in itself unreasonable – but it shouldn't be taken for granted that Sappho's poems are always the products of entirely personal occasions. Much ancient lyric poetry was composed for ceremonial occasions of various kinds, whether for use in actual public ceremonies or rites or in some more private way. Although there is no record of Sappho composing, like Alkman, choral odes to be sung by several voices, the solo songs which were her *forte* may often be poems in which the singer is not Sappho in her own voice, but a real or imagined other person. Or persons, since there is evidence that Sappho wrote at least one poem for two or more characters.

We can only consider Sappho's poetry now as literature, and that is perhaps as great a loss as the physical loss of more than ninety per cent of her verse. She wrote her poems for singing, accompanied by the *kithara* or *barbitos*, usually translated as 'lyre'. (She is also credited with the invention of a new kind of lyre, the *plektron*.) It is this sense of lyre which is at the root of 'lyric' in our phrase 'lyric poetry'. But our post-Romantic, post-modern sense of lyric poetry is little more than poetry with a personal theme or subject, in some approximation or shadow of a stanza form. Of Sappho's lyric work we can safely say that she wrote her own verse and music, played her own instrument and sometimes sang her own songs: and that we have almost no idea what they sounded like.

And so to the endless speculation, with a few hard facts first. We know that she wrote marriage-songs: Book 9 of the Alexandrian edition, which arranged her poems by metre, collected them. Her poetry was largely solo lyric, but she wrote at least one poem in dialogue form for worshippers of Adonis. Ancient writers who knew her entire written work make it plain that it was mostly love poetry. Her immediate audience was her circle of friends, women and girls, or at least this is plausibly suggested by the fragment: 'I shall now sing these songs beautifully to delight my companions' (fr. 160). She speaks lovingly of a daughter (but *pais*, as Mary Lefkowitz points out, can mean slave as well as child). Her brother Charaxos, a trader, spent a lot of money on a woman called Doricha, who lived in Egypt: Sappho chides him in poems. Slightly less hard fact: she may have had pupils, whether formally or informally, as is suggested by fr. 150's reference to 'the house of those who serve the Muses'. An anonymous commentator writes in a mid-second-century AD papyrus that while civil war was raging Sappho 'taught in peace and quiet the noblest girls not only of local families but also of Ionian ones' – that is, from the western seaboard of Asia Minor.

In the Byzantine lexicon known as the *Suda*, a massive and unreliable collection of folklore, there are two entries on Sappho. The first reads: 'Daughter of Simon. Other say of Eumenos, or Eërygyios, or Ekrytos, or Semos, or Kamon, or Etarchos, or Skamandronymos. Kleïs was her mother. A Lesbian from Eresos, a lyric poet. Active in the 42nd Olympiad [612–608 BC], the time of Alkaios, Stesichoros and Pittakos. She had three brothers, Larichos, Charaxos and Eurygios. Married to a very wealthy man, Kerkylas, a trader from Andros, by whom she had a daughter called Kleïs. She had three close companions, Atthis, Telesippa and Megara, and got a bad reputation for her impure relationships with them. Her pupils were Anagora from Miletus, Gongyla from Colophon, Euneika from Salamis. She wrote 9 books of lyric poems, and invented the *plektron*. She also wrote inscriptions, elegies, iambic poems and solo songs.'

The second takes a quite different tack: 'A Lesbian from Mytilene, a lyre-player. This Sappho drowned herself from the cliff of Leukates for love of Phaon the Mytilenean. Some say that she was a lyric poet too.'

One may as well say at once that the legend of Sappho's suicide for love of Phaon (the name means 'Shining') is a bit of nonsense that has bedevilled Sappho's presence in literature ever since its invention, possibly by a playwright in the era of the Middle Comedy of the fourth century BC, which spawned six comedies called *Sappho*, two called *Phaon* and at least five on *Leukas* or *The Leukadian*, all lost. Even in ancient times Sappho was the stuff of legend. It is reported that the comic playwright Diphilos made her the lover of Archilochos and Hipponax (two roughly contemporary poets from other parts of the Greek world). Greek comedy had a penchant for scurrilous or burlesque treatment of famous historical characters, and this is a case where the mud has stuck. And we are stuck with the myth of Phaon, tedious fiction though it is, as part of Sappho's presence in English.

It is probably to get round this and to salvage Sappho's reputation that the idea of the two Sapphos was concocted. In the early second century AD, Aelian noted: 'I gather that there was another Sappho in Lesbos, a courtesan not a poet.' This idea also resurfaces in the *Suda* entry on Phaon: 'they say that Phaon was loved by many women, including Sappho – not the poet but another Lesbian – who threw herself from the Leukadian cliff when he spurned her.'

Little of the folklore about Sappho is worth reporting in a book which tries to focus on the poetry, but one may as well mention one other piece of tradition which has come down, in the form of an anonymous commentator's footnote on a passage in Lucian's *Portraits*. 'Physically Sappho was very ugly. She was small and dark, like a nightingale with shapeless wings enfolding a tiny body.' This tradition must go back a long way; it is evident in Ovid's poem about Sappho and Phaon in the *Heroides*, and is the source of Swinburne's 'the small dark body's Lesbian loveliness / That held the fire eternal'.

All this speculation is nicely put in its place by Seneca in one of his *Letters.* 'The scholar Didymus wrote four thousand books. I would pity him if he'd read as many useless works. Among them you find enquiries into Homer's birthplace, Aeneas's real mother, whether Anacreon was more of a womanizer than a drunk, whether Sappho was a prostitute, and other things worth forgetting if you knew them. Go on, tell me that life is not long!'

More interesting than all this is what Sappho's poetry meant first to the ancient Greeks, then to the Romans; and what it has meant in English (which until relatively recently has depended on the Romans, especially Ovid). Sappho's poetry was categorized by the Alexandrian scholars – who one must suppose had her complete works – into nine books, each book being a roll of about 30 feet containing on average perhaps 500 or 600 lines. (Book I in fact contained 1320 lines, i.e. 330 Sapphic stanzas; Book 8 a mere 130 or 140 lines.) Roman poets like Catullus and Horace who were familiar with her work nearly 600 years after her time could have read it all. But at some point in late antiquity, the bulk of her work disappears. The sixteenth-century scholar Scaliger placed the destruction of Sappho's poems as late as 1073 AD, when bonfires were made at Rome and Constantinople of the poems of Sappho and other 'heathen singers', under Pope Gregory VII. What we have now, less than a tenth, is a mixture of quotations by ancient writers and papyrus finds, often shredded, many of them recent: some Oxyrhyncus papyrus fragments of Sappho were being deciphered and printed in the 1910s, and more have come to light since.

Catullus famously imitated the Sappho poem which is known to us through quotation by Longinus, if that is really the name of the author of *Peri Hypsous*, generally mistranslated 'On the Sublime' but more accurately 'On elevated style' or 'On great writing'. This is a work of uncertain date; it is most likely of the first, but possibly the third century AD. 'Sappho,' he wrote, 'for example, always picks out the emotions associated with erotic delirium from the components of the situation in real life. How does she demonstrate her virtuosity? In her skilful selection and blending of the most important and intense details.' After quoting the poem he points out that she conveys 'not a single emotion but an assembly of emotions.'

There is little ancient criticism which is as much to the point as this, although Dionysios of Halikarnassos, the first-century BC historian who moved to Rome and to whom we owe the preservation of Sappho's only certainly complete poem, the ode to Aphrodite, says of it in his *Literary Composition*: 'The harmony and grace of this piece lie in the continuity and smoothness of its construction. Words are set next to others and interwoven with them according to certain natural affinities and groupings of letters...'

But Catullus was imitating, not translating, and has a fourth stanza owing nothing to Sappho. There are other Sapphic echoes in his work, notably in his poems 61 and 62, and none so pervasive as the fact that he gave the woman who is the object of so many of the love-poems, almost certainly to be identified with Clodia Metelli, the pseudonym Lesbia. There may be lost, private reasons for this choice, but to those outside Catullus' and Clodia's circle the soubriquet would have been redolent of poetic-erotic refinement and not of Lesbianism in the modern sense. In another playful reference in poem 35, Catullus forgives his friend Caecilius's girl-friend for being in love with a poet who has made such a wonderful start to his long poem: 'ignosco tibi, Sapphica puella / musa doctior': she knows more about poetry than Sappho.

Both Catullus and Horace used Sappho's stanza form, and Horace too pays her elegant implicit compliments. But though his *Odes* 4.9 shows that he understood Sappho's special erotic spell, *Odes* 2.13 makes it clear that for Horace, Sappho's Lesbian contemporary Alkaios was the poet who echoed most strongly.

> *Aeoliis fidibus querentem*
> *Sappho puellis de popularibus,*
> *et te sonantem plenius aureo,*
> *Alcaee, plectro dura navis,*
> *dura fugae mala, dura belli!*

'Sappho complaining to her Aeolian lyre about the girls of her city; and you, Alkaios, more resonantly sounding with your gold *plektron* the hardships of your boat, the evil hardships of exile, the hardships of war.' Ovid concurred that 'grandius ille sonet', he resounds more grandly, which is probably as much a comment on Alkaios's themes as on his style.

Of Alkaios's poetry we have about as much as of Sappho's. Much of his poetry was to do with the convoluted politics of Lesbos and the tyranny of the Pittakos or Myrsilos clans, of which in Sappho we hear nothing. Alkaios was also a forerunner of Anakreon in his penchant for 'drink for tomorrow we die' or 'carpe diem' songs. Scholars have difficulty in assigning some of the papyrus fragments to Alkaios or to Sappho, because they shared the Aiolic dialect and often wrote in the same metres.

This aside serves to remind us that the taste for one kind of poetry or another depends largely on the needs of later readers, and in the Augustan period the question of poetry's relationship to imperial power was a very real issue. The poets relied on their patrons: Vergil, Propertius and Horace, Maecenas's poets, were under pressure to write what he and his friend the Emperor thought Roman literature, or the Augustan empire, needed.

It also reminds us that the Lesbos of Sappho's and Alkaios's time was not only sophisticated but also turbulent. Whether or not the story of Sappho's supposed exile to Sicily (perhaps in her child-hood, because of political turmoil in Lesbos) is true, whether or not she and Alkaios as fellow-poets were on close terms, we cannot tell.

In an Epistle (1.19) Horace writes:

> *temperat Archilochi musam pede mascula Sappho,*
> *temperat Alcaeus, sed rebus et ordine dispar...*

'Masculine Sappho moderates the muse of Archilochus in her metre, so does Alkaios, but he differs in themes and arrangement.' If Horace's choice of adjective seems strange or provocative, here are two ancient explanations: 'Sappho is "mascula",' according to Porphyrio's commentary, 'either because she is famous for her poetry, in which more often men are, or because she is defamed as having been a tribade.' Another writer, Dionysius Latinus, glosses Horace's *mascula* as 'not soft [in our contemporary sense of 'gay'], nor destroyed by dissolution nor unchaste.'

Sappho's actual sexuality, whether personal or poetic (which may or may not be the same) is one thing. We cannot possibly deduce much about it from our sketchy knowledge of the conven-tions of Lesbian society at the time, or from the fragments of Sappho's poems. Some scholars believe they can make out the word *olisbos* (dildo) in a very fragmentary papyrus in which little is certain: see Guy Davenport's speculative version on p. 77. Her perceived sexuality, however, and its influence are another. It is this which has made Sappho an icon for lesbians and feminists in the past hundred or so years.

The rot in Sappho's reputation, the travesty of her image which began with the Greek comic playwrights, starts from our point of view with Ovid, because he was such an influential writer for

English poets of the sixteenth and seventeenth centuries. Ovid intended no sneer when he wrote 'Lesbia quid docuit Sappho, nisi amare, puellas?' – 'What did Sappho of Lesbos teach girls, except how to love?' (*Tristia* 2. 365): he pinpoints an important strand in her poetry, we would suggest as important morally as erotically. The context helps:

quid, nisi cum multo Uenerem confundere uino,
praecepit lyrici Teia Musa senis?
Lesbia quid docuit Sappho, nisi amare, puellas?

'What precepts did the Teian Muse of the old lyric poet [Anakreon] give, except how to mix Love with a lot of wine? What did Sappho of Lesbos teach girls, except how to love?'

Many views have been taken of the relations between Sappho and her intimate circle. Sappho has been presented as the head-mistress of a girls' academy or cultural finishing-school, leader and chief composer for a girl's choir, a sort of cult priestess with female acolytes, poet in residence of a female writers' workshop... and a dozen other things, all more or less solemnly propounded on the thinnest of evidence by generations of scholars. Arthur S. Way, a verse translator of the old school, wrote in 1920: 'Readers who know something of the passionate attachments between girls at school and college, of their adoration for each other and their teachers, will not think it strange that we find evidence in these poems of similar links of love between Sappho and some of her girl-students. ... Human nature has not changed in five-and-twenty centuries.'

Rather more relevantly, Maximus of Tyre, an itinerant lecturer and writer of the second century AD, has this to say on the subject of the quality of Sappho's relationships: 'What else was the Lesbian's love but the art of love as practised by Sokrates? They both seem to me to have engaged in their own kind of love, she of women, he of men. Both said that they loved many and that they were captivated by all beauty. What Alkibiades, Charmides and Phaidros were to him, Gyrinna, Atthis and Anaktoria were to her; and what his rival practitioners, Prodikos, Gorgias, Thrasymachos and Protagoras were to Sokrates, so Gorgo and Andromeda were to Sappho. Sometimes she reproaches them, or cross-questions them, and she uses irony exactly like Sokrates.'

We can claim, this side of rashness, that she was a poet, composer and singer. Like Alkaios, she was a Lesbian. And she was lesbian, a fact which bothered the more perceptive of the ancients, who had read all her work, not at all. As a character remarks in Plutarch's *Pythian Oracles*: 'Don't you see what charm Sappho's songs have to entice and enchant the listener?' Or as Demetrius in his work on style said simply: 'The charm is in the subjects, such as the nymphs' gardens, the wedding-songs, love-affairs, the whole poetry of Sappho.'

WHAT ARE THE qualities of Sappho's poetry, in so far as they can be judged on so little evidence? Apart from those which we have already mentioned, and which were evident to the ancients, there are a few simple points one can make, although they cannot easily be substantiated to Greekless readers. She has a wonderful ear: the poetry is musical, more so than that of her contemporary Alkaios, even without the music. Only Alkman approaches her in this. Although it is not a technical quality, she has a lovely sense of humour and is incapable of over-solemnity (this defeats most of her translators). Perhaps human qualities are, after all, technical qualities in the right hands. Her ability to modulate diction and move deftly from a formal mode to an intimate one over the course of a few stanzas is unique in Greek. The ode to Aphrodite begins grandly and memorably with a first line of three measured polysyllables – *Poikilothron' athanat' Aphrodita* – but in the fifth stanza we have a colloquial passage in which the goddess addresses and ironically berates her. This shift is delicately done: it is witty in the best sense.

What Dionysius meant about her words being juxtaposed and interwoven according to 'certain natural affinities and groupings of letters' is not entirely clear, since he does not give specific examples, but he may have had in mind something like what happens in the opening six lines of *Phainetai moi* (see p. 28). It is almost an onomatopoeic or mimetic use of language: the placement of the adjective *himeroën* in line 5 with its sudden shimmying rhythm, like a chuckle, between a succession of deliciously dwelt-on long syllables and diphthongs; and the practically audible flutter on the stressed first syllable of *eptoaisen* at the end of line 6. No doubt she was not always this marvellous, but nobody ever complained that she wrote badly.

SAPPHO IS ALMOST AN open book with many blank pages. So little is known for certain that poets have felt that they may remake her in any image they choose. Probably the first bit of English translation of a Sappho fragment is a line by Ben Jonson in his play *The Sad Shepherd*: 'The dear good Angel of the spring, the nightingale'. Greek was less read than Latin until the eighteenth century, and texts were scarce. Sappho's first substantial appearance in English is as the Princess of Syracuse in John Lyly's prose play *Sapho and Phao* (1584), in which her poetry or even its existence plays no part. (Another strange play on the Sappho/Phaon theme is Lawrence Durrell's verse-drama of 1950, *Sappho*, which is again irrelevant to any consideration of her poetry. More entertaining is Peter Green's Sappho novel, *The Laughter of Aphrodite*, 1988.)

The first serious critical appreciation of Sappho in English was by Joseph Addison, writing in *Spectator* no. 223 (1711), in which the first of Ambrose Philips' translations appeared.

> Among the mutilated Poets of Antiquity, there is none whose Fragments are so beautiful as those of *Sappho*. They give us a Taste of her way of Writing, which is perfectly conformable with that extraordinary Character we find of her, in the Remarks of those great Criticks who were conversant with her Works when they were entire. One may see, by what is left of them, that she followed Nature in all her Thoughts, without descending to those little Points, Conceits, and Turns of Wit with which many of our Modern Lyricks are so miserably infected. Her Soul seems to have been made up of Love and Poetry: She felt the Passion in all its Warmth, and described it in all its Symptoms... I do not know, by the Character that is given of her Works, whether it is not for the Benefit of Mankind that they are lost. They were filled with such bewitching Tenderness and Rapture, that it might have been dangerous to have given them a reading.

Nevertheless, to our ears Sappho sounds faintly ridiculous in seventeenth- and eighteenth-century English garb. This is partly because of the then prevailing idea that poetry ought to be elevated and ornamental in style. (The opposite – and still prevalent – idea, that it should be level and plain, has its own drawbacks.) The Sapphic stanza never really did become naturalized in English. Pope essayed a schoolboy attempt to write Sapphics, but earlier attempts were fairly stumbling, and it is not until Swinburne that the Sapphic stanza in English begins to sound at all plausible.

In 'Notes on Poems and Reviews' Swinburne explains why he felt unable to translate Sappho's poems, but hoped with 'Anactoria' to convey his sense of her poetry. 'I tried then to write some paraphrase of the fragments which the Fates and the Christians have spared us…. No one can feel more deeply than I do the inadequacy of my work. "That is not Sappho" a friend once said to me. I could only reply, "It is as near as I can come; and no man can come close to her." Her remaining verses are the supreme success, the final achievement, of the poetic art…. I have striven to cast my spirit into the mould of hers, to express and represent not the poem but the poet.'

Like his contemporary John Addington Symonds, he had a keen awareness of her unparalleled quality. 'Judging even from the mutilated fragments fallen within our reach from the broken altar of her sacrifice of song, I for one have always agreed with all Grecian tradition in thinking Sappho to be beyond all question and comparison the very greatest poet that ever lived.' Swinburne was a good hellenist, and his opinion, in conjunction with Symonds' extensive and erudite writings on Greek poetry – their sensibility is similar – marks the beginning of the modern, post-Romantic appreciation of Sappho's poetry. Quite why the Romantic poets, and Shelley in particular, did not co-opt Sappho for their cause is a slight mystery.

HOWEVER ONE MIGHT wish it otherwise, historians and critics of English poetry have until recently assumed a canon of poets in which men had a huge numeric advantage. On a practical level, this assumption has been redressed in recent years by poetry anthologies such as Roger Lonsdale's *Eighteenth-Century Women Poets* and *Victorian Women Poets* by Angela Leighton and Margaret Reynolds. Literary historians are still trying to investigate the conditions in which women wrote and published poetry and how those conditions were determined by gender and social class. It's obvious that few (even well-connected) women poets were educated classicists before the twentieth century and actually getting to publish work was often difficult and unsupported. The idea of open (and paid) publication for a woman writer was often socially akin to prostitution. Educated women had other pursuits to attend to, as Elizabeth Moody ironically demonstrated in 'Sappho Burns her Books and Cultivates the Culinary Arts'. Germaine Greer's recent book *Slip-Shod Sibyls* traces much of this, and has an entertaining and informative chapter on Sappho's reception in English especially by women.

In 1683 Aphra Behn congratulated Thomas Creech on his translation of Lucretius' *De Rerum Natura* and complained about the inaccessibility of Greek and Roman authors to English women:

> *Till now I curst my* Sex *and* Education,
> *And more the scanted Customs of the Nation,*
> *Permitting not the Female Sex to tread*
> *The Mighty Paths of Learned* Heroes *Dead.*
> *The Godlike* Virgil *and Great* Homers *Muse*
> *Like Divine Mysteries are conceal'd from us...*

(To the Unknown DAPHNIS on his Excellent Translation of *Lucretius*)

Aphra Behn probably had little knowledge of Sappho's poems in spite of frequent comparisons between the two women in dedicatory epistles to Behn's work. Almost two hundred years later, Lucy Snowe, the central character of Charlotte Brontë's *Villette*, underwent quite extraordinary humiliation at the hands of a potential suitor because he suspected her of concealing a knowledge of Greek and Latin. Lucy Snowe confesses that at moments 'I *did* wish that his suspicions had been better founded. There were times when I would have given my right hand to possess the treasures he ascribed to me.' Most of the pre-twentieth-century women poets in this anthology were probably Greekless. Many women writers came to Sappho through translations of Ovid's *Sappho to Phaon* or read versions of Sappho's poetry which deliberately changed the sex of the love object. Until Wharton's *Sappho* which printed Symonds's 1883 translation, the ode to Aphrodite was a plea to the Cyprian goddess to help entrap some unspecified male figure. Although many translations of Ovid's *Sappho to Phaon* retained references to Sappho's feelings for 'the Lesbian Dames', the trend was towards the Phaon love story. Francis Fawkes even decided to weave Phaon into his translation of the ode and blur the distinction between the Ovidian myth of Sappho and her poetry even further.

It isn't surprising that most of the poetry written by women about Sappho (at least up until the end of the nineteenth century) re-worked the story about Sappho's suicidal love for Phaon. Fragment 94, an erotic dialogue between Sappho and a young woman which would have been difficult to heterosexualize, wasn't discovered until the beginning of the twentieth century. Any woman poet who wanted to investigate Sappho's poetry had either to arm herself with Greek or accept a body of work refracted through countless Roman and English male translators, mythologizers and editors. Victorian women poets who might have had some knowledge of ancient Greek tended to fillet Sappho's poems for occasional lines to start their own poems: none made sustained translations. Katherine Bradley and Edith Cooper, writing as Michael Field, used epigraphs drawn from Sappho's fragments for their own homoerotic poems. Their book *Long Ago* was published in 1889, a few years after the first edition of Wharton's work.

The American classicist Mary Barnard was the first woman to translate Sappho's fragments: her version appeared in 1958. Ezra Pound had encouraged her in letters as far back as 1934 to translate Sappho as practice for her poetry. ('You hate translation??? What of it?? Expect to be carried up Mt. Helicon in an easy chair?') In the introduction to her translations she demolished the more scurrilous biographical myths about Sappho but steered clear of making any controversial statements about the male writers who created them. Barnard does, however, argue about the nature of Sappho's relationships with the named women in her fragments. Although her introduction is robust, she claims to be taking sides in a dispute between two grand old men of scholarship (Denys Page and Maurice Bowra) on whether Sappho had an official rôle in the education of the young girls mentioned in her fragments. Barnard is anxious to promote the image of a bluestocking Sappho and states, 'I myself should prefer, however, to compare Sappho's entirely hypothetical position to that of *kapelmeister*, or perhaps to that of a Renaissance painter with a studio full of talented young fellows picking up the tricks of painting alterpieces.' The lesbian content of Sappho's poems seems to have no specifically female cultural space: Sappho's relationships are translated into images of male artists (the Renaissance painter) and the feelings men have for each other when producing great works of art.

Josephine Balmer's *Sappho: Poems and Fragments* (1984) was the first complete set of translations by a woman to ask consciously feminist questions about how Sappho has been received and translated. She asks, with reference to the work of Mary Lefkowitz, why Sappho's poems – and women's writing as a whole – seem to be read as thinly veiled autobiography. Germaine Greer's *Slip-Shod Sibyls* interrogates notions of text and authorship in relation to Sappho, and other feminist scholars like Margaret Reynolds and Emma Donoghue have worked on detailed studies of Sappho in an eighteenth- and nineteenth-century context.

Towards the end of the eighteenth century, women poets started to use the Sappho story in their own poetry. Mary Robinson – to whom Coleridge's 'Alcaeus to Sappho' (p. 103) may well be addressed – wrote a long sonnet sequence titled *Sappho and Phaon* in 1796. Her Sappho is cast firmly in the literary mood of sensibility which dominated the second half of the eighteenth century. Robinson prefixes her poems with a short essay which testifies to Sappho's 'vivid glow of sensibility' and the exquisite 'taste, feeling and inspiration' of her poems. She concludes her introduction with a rather euphemistic discussion of Sappho's literary reputation:

> If her writings were, in some instances, too glowing for the fastidious refinement of modern times; let it be her excuse, and the honour of her country, that the liberal education of the Greeks was such, as inspired them with an unprejudiced enthusiasm for the works of genius: and that when they paid adoration to Sappho, they idolized the MUSE, and not the WOMAN.

Robinson doesn't vindicate Sappho personally, but quotes extensively from a French work by Abbe Barthelemi which suggests that Sappho's homoerotic tendencies and her passion for Phaon were the result of 'extreme sensibility'. Female sensibility was under interrogation from writers as diverse as Mary Wollstonecraft and the young Jane Austen during the 1790s, and Robinson's Sappho was both a representation of the literary phenomena and a warning against its dangers to the sanity of women.

Nineteenth-century women poets like Felicia Hemans, Caroline Norton and Laetitia Elizabeth Landon took up the Sappho and Phaon story with particular emphasis on Sappho's suicide (L.E.L. did actually commit suicide). Christina Rossetti's poem 'What Sappho would have said had her leap cured instead of killing her' is an interesting departure from the prevailing suicide-note poem. The poem's argument resembles a seventeenth-century metaphysical poem about love and retirement with a powerfully erotic energy. By the end of the nineteenth century, the Sappho and Phaon story had lost its hold over women poets writing about Sappho.

WITH THE CANADIAN poet Bliss Carman, whose *Sappho: One Hundred Lyrics* (1910) was a huge success, we have the meeting of a late-Romantic with an almost Georgian, just pre-imagist sensibility. This is Sappho out of Ernest Dowson. We have put his poems in section 2, although they often include much straightforward translation. But he was attempting to produce a rounded fictional portrait in his poem-cycle, and fiction – especially with his emphasis on the god Pan – triumphs over known historical fact.

His Sappho, like that of Ambrose Philips, is still on a pedestal. She begins to come down to earth with the version by Richard Aldington which Pound admired. Pound himself wrote a poem (p. 135; the title means 'I desire') which owes something both to Sappho and to Aldington, and other poems in *Lustra* (1915) show traces of this kind of imagistic hellenism. He also has a three-line poem called 'Papyrus' which is actually direct translation from a Sappho papyrus, but was presumably intended as an imagist fragment in its own right. Guy Davenport quotes it, without the ellipses after each word and with Gongula differently spelt, in the opening of his no. 8 (p. 74). A detailed account of the Imagists' attraction to Sappho, and Pound's use of her poetry, is given by Hugh Kenner in his essay 'The Muse in Tatters'.

Richard Aldington was a much younger man than Carman when he did his version, only a few years after the publication of Carman's *Sappho*, a book which Pound studiously refrained from mentioning: whenever he did recommend a Sappho in English, it was the solidly Victorian Wharton's compilation (a 'classic achievement', he wrote in a 1916 letter). But in a way there is not such a huge gap between Carman and Aldington. Both are seduced by sound and rhythm, and by an intangibly mystic aura which the poems seem to have for them: a kind of Grecian twilight. Mary Barnard's translation is perhaps the first that strips this away completely, but one may now feel that she goes too far in a prosaic, or perhaps one should say 'non-lyric' – remembering the strict sense of lyric – direction.

The shift in emphasis between Carman and Aldington is subtle but distinct. Aldington was married to H.D., another imagist, a better poet than him and a good hellenist. Surprisingly, however, H.D. – who did translate a number of extracts from Greek tragedies, and embedded versions of several Greek epigrams in other poems – never directly translates or adapts any piece of Sappho. The nearest she comes is by alluding to Sappho in epigraphs to a handful of poems, in her collections *Hymen* (1921) and *Heliodora*, 1924. 'The four Sappho fragments are reworked freely', she says, but it is less than that: she uses them only as points of departure for poems which move in completely non-Sapphic directions. In this way she succeeds in avoiding creative dialogue with Sappho entirely.

H.D. was perhaps too preoccupied with her own standing as a woman poet to wish to follow a route apparently ordained for her by Pound and Aldington. She did, however, write a curious essay, 'The Wise Sappho', which was published in 1957. It is a personal and poetic homage, almost at times a prose-poem. H.D. begins: '"Little, but all roses" is the dictate of the Alexandrine poet, yet I am inclined to disagree.' Her version of Meleager's famous phrase about Sappho's poems (from the introductory poem to his anthology *The Garland*) runs like a refrain through the piece, and she plays on shades of meaning of the word 'little'. But there is a problem with her reading of his description of the 'Sappho' epigrams: *baia men alla rhoda* is normally understood as 'few, but roses'. It is hard to see that he could have meant 'little', since the two epigrams attributed to Sappho, though of two and four lines, are only little by modern standards: their length is typical for the genre. His anthology contained no lyric verse, only epigrams.

The history of the struggles of women writers to establish their own course, their own identity, and to be taken seriously, is another story which feminist historians have begun to map out. But these remarks may help to explain why there are fewer women poets and translators in this book than we would like.

WE HOPE THAT this collection traces a clear outline of Sappho's presence in English poetry and the uses to which her ever-fertile poetry has been put. We hope too that readers can piece together, from so many versions of her over so many years, their own authentic Sappho. It will be necessarily fragmentary, as even a 'complete' version is. The fragmentary nature of Sappho's remnants, especially in the recent papyrus discoveries, is something which no poetic translator had fully addressed until Guy Davenport (1965).

We have arranged the poets chronologically by birth, although this has some curious consequences: William Carlos Williams, whose version was published in 1957, appears before Richard Aldington, whose poem was published some forty years earlier. The arrangement of the anthology into two sections distinguishes between translation and 'treatments', but the distinction is not hard and fast. We have put Mary Barnard in the first and Bliss Carman in the second section, but aspects of the work of each could well appear in the other part. In Part Two, Thomas Moore's 'Evenings in Greece' (p. 106) embeds the translation in an imagined domestic drama, while Swinburne weaves patches of near-translation into both 'Sapphics' and 'Anactoria' (p. 116 ff).

To a general rule of no translations from other poets besides Ovid we have made two exceptions, not counting Sir Philip Sidney's poem which may derive from the Catullus version. Edwin Arlington Robinson's beautiful 'Doricha', from the Greek of the third-century BC epigrammatist Poseidippos, may stand as an emblem for the many poems about Sappho in *The Greek Anthology*, and the many other ancient poems about her that are lost, while Olga Broumas and Jane Miller's version from Pierre Louÿs's *Chansons de Bilitis* (1894) – fictional translations from a woman poet contemporary with Sappho – is movingly Sapphic in spirit.

We have not been able to offer versions of all of Sappho's better-known fragments, but hope that the pleasure of comparison of different approaches to the same important poems makes up for this. We have deliberately printed many fewer versions from the last fifty years than from previous periods, because modern versions are more accessible – half a dozen are in print – while many of the older ones have not been reprinted this century.

For other omissions, if not for our ignorance, we plead a shortage of pages. We could easily have printed more Michael Field, Swinburne ('On the Cliffs'), Landor, Felicia Hemans ('Genius Singing to Love'), Sara Teasdale ('Erinna', and the second and third parts of 'Sappho'), Bliss Carman... and so on. There are good versions by such contemporary poets as John Heath-Stubbs, John Frederick Nims, Sam Hamill, the late Tom Scott and Sydney Goodsir Smith. Elijah Fenton's *Phaon to Sappho* was tempting as a reversal of the usual Ovid-based treatment, but we were suffering from an excess of Phaonics.

Some poems – notably the two 'Sappho' epigrams about Meniscus and Timas, and the little lyric about midnight and time passing – are now no longer attributed to Sappho by any scholars: the epigrams because many were fraudulently or mistakenly attributed to Sappho in ancient times, regardless of dialect, and the lyric again because it is not in Aiolic. It is most likely a fragment of a folk-song.

PETER JAY
CAROLINE LEWIS

A Brief Bibliography

PARALLEL TEXT

Greek Lyric, vol. I: Sappho and Alcaeus, with an English
  translation by David A. Campbell: Loeb Classical Library,
  Cambridge, Mass. and London, 1982

SOME MODERN TRANSLATIONS

Josephine Balmer, *Sappho: Poems and Fragments*, London, 1984
  and Newcastle, 1992
Mary Barnard, *Sappho*, Berkeley and Los Angeles, 1958
Willis Barnstone, *Greek Lyric Poetry*, New York, 1967
Guy Davenport, *Sappho: Poems and Fragments*, Ann Arbor, 1965
Suzy Q. Groden, *The Poems of Sappho*, Library of Liberal Arts:
  Indianapolis, 1966
Jim Powell, *Sappho: A Garland*, New York, 1993
Paul Roche, *The Love Songs of Sappho*, Toronto, 1966
M. L. West, *Greek Lyric Poetry*, World's Classics: Oxford, 1993

MISCELLANEOUS

C. M. Bowra, *Greek Lyric Poetry*, 2nd edition, Oxford, 1961
Anne Pippin Burnett, *Three Archaic Poets* (Archilochus, Alcaeus,
  Sappho), London, 1983
Emma Donoghue, *Passions Between Women: British Lesbian Culture
  1668–1801*, London, 1993
Page duBois, *Sappho is Burning*, Chicago, 1995
Germaine Greer, 'The Enigma of Sappho', chapter 4 of *Slip-Shod
  Sibyls*, London, 1995
Hugh Kenner, 'The Muse in Tatters'; *Arion* vol. 7, 1968 and *Agenda*
  vol. 6.2, 1968; reprinted in the Penguin critical anthologies
  series, *Ezra Pound*, ed. J. P. Sullivan, Harmondsworth, 1970
Margaret Reynolds, 'I Lived for Art, I Lived for Love; the Woman
  Poet Sings Sappho's Last Song', in *Victorian Women Poets:
  A Critical Reader*, ed. Angela Leighton, Oxford, 1996
Margaret Reynolds, *The Sappho Companion*, London, 2000
June Mackintosh Snyder, *Women and the Lyre*, Bristol, 1989
Margaret Williamson, *Sappho's Immortal Daughters*, New Haven
  and London, 1995

SAPPHO

φαίνεταί μοι κῆνος ἴσος θέοισιν
ἔμμεν' ὤνηρ, ὄττις ἐνάντιός τοι
ἰσδάνει καὶ πλάσιον ἆδυ φωνεί-
σας ὑπακούει   4

καὶ γελαίσας ἰμέροεν, τό μ' ἦ μὰν
καρδίαν ἐν στήθεσιν ἐπτόαισεν·
ὡς γὰρ ἐς σ' ἴδω βρόχε', ὥς με φώναι-
σ' οὐδ' ἒν ἔτ' εἴκει,   8

ἀλλὰ κὰμ μὲν γλῶσσά μ' ἔαγε, λέπτον
δ' αὔτικα χρῷ πῦρ ὐπαδεδρόμηκεν,
ὀππάτεσσι δ' οὐδ' ἒν ὄρημμ', ἐπιρρόμ-
βεισι δ' ἄκουαι,   12

κὰδ δέ μ' ἴδρως κακχέεται, τρόμος δὲ
παῖσαν ἄγρει, χλωροτέρα δὲ ποίας
ἔμμι, τεθνάκην δ' ὀλίγω 'πιδεύης
φαίνομ' ἔμ' αὔτᾳ.   16

ἀλλὰ πὰν τόλματον ἐπεὶ καὶ πένητα ...

Note on text (above)

The Greek text given here is based on
D. A. Campbell's Loeb edition. Read-
ings in lines 9 and 13 are particularly
uncertain; common alternatives (often
translated in this book) are:

LINE 9

ἀλλ' ἄκαν μὲν γλῶσσα ϝέαγε, λέπτον
but my tongue [or: speech] sticks [or:
    breaks], subtle

LINE 13

κὰδ δέ μ' ἴδρως ψῦχρος ἔχει, τρόμος δὲ
over me a cold sweat pours down,
    trembling

Note on transcription (opposite)

METRICAL SCHEME

$- \smile \ | - \underline{\smile} \ | - \smile \smile \ | - \smile \ | - \underline{\smile} \ $ [x 3]
$- \smile \smile \ | - -$

PRONUNCIATION

e = eta, long e
o = omega, long o
y = upsilon, close to French 'u'
ai roughly as in 'sky'
ei roughly as in 'way'
g hard as in 'get'
ch as in 'loch', 'echt'
All diphthongs are long
Diaereses show that two vowels are
    pronounced separately
Long syllables only are marked

Phainetai moi kenos isos theoisin
Seems to me that (man) level with the gods
emmen' oner, hottis enantios toi
to be (that) man, who opposite you
isdanei kai plasion ady phonei-
sits and close-up (your) sweet speak-
sas hypakouei
ing listens to

kai gelaisas himeroën, to m' e man
and laughter lovely [or: joyful], which (made) truly my
kardian en stethesin eptoaisen.
heart in (my) breast flutter.
Os gar es s' ido broche', os me phonai-
When in-fact at you I look briefly, then for me speaking
s' oud' en et' eikei,
no longer is possible,

alla kam men glossa m' eäge, lepton
but my tongue [or: speech] sticks, subtle
d' autika chro(ï) pyr ypadedromeken,
then (under) my skin a fire has run under,
oppatessi d' oud' en oremm', epirrhom-
with (my) eyes nothing I see, hum
beisi d' akouai,
(my) ears,

kad de m' idros kakcheëtai, tromos de
over me sweat pours down, trembling
paisan agrei, chlorotera de poias
all-over grips (me), paler than grass
emmi, tethnaken d' oligo 'pideues
I am, of dying little lacking
phainom' em' auta(ï).
I seem [to be to myself].

Alla pan tolmaton epei kai peneta
But all must be endured since a poor...

CATULLUS

LI

Ille mi par esse deo uidetur,
ille, si fas est, superare diuos,
qui sedens aduersus identidem te
    spectat et audit

dulce ridentem, misero quod omnis
eripit sensus mihi: nam simul te,
Lesbia, aspexi, nihil est super mi
    [vocis in ore]

lingua sed torpet, tenuis sub artus
flamma demanat, sonitu suopte
tintinant aures, gemina teguntur
    lumina nocte.

otium, Catulle, tibi molestum est:
otio exsultas nimiumque gestis:
otium et reges prius et beatas
    perdidit urbes.

*That man seems to me on a par with God, to be (if it's
permissible) superior to the gods, who sitting opposite you
continually sees and hears you*
    *sweetly laughing – that tore all the senses from me, poor
fool: for as soon, Lesbia, as I caught sight of you, nothing [of
speech in my mouth] is left me,*
    *but my tongue is paralysed, a subtle flame flows
through my limbs, my ears ring with sound of their own,
my eyes are covered in night.*
    *Free time is bad for you, Catullus; free time makes you
restless and over-excited; free time before now has ruined
kings and prosperous cities.*

I

VERSIONS

TRANSLATIONS AND IMITATIONS

SIR PHILIP SIDNEY

'*My muse, what ails this ardour?*'

My muse, what ails this ardour?
My eys be dym, my lymns shake,
My voice is hoarse, my throte scorcht,
My tong to this roofe cleaves,
My fancy amazde, my thoughtes dull'd,
My head doth ake, my life faints,
My sowle begins to take leave,
So greate a passion all feele,
To think a soare so deadly
I should so rashly ripp up.

JOHN HALL

'He that sits next to thee ...'

He that sits next to thee now and hears
Thy charming voyce, to me appears
Beauteous as any Deity
        That rules the skie.

How did his pleasing glances dart
Sweet languors to my ravish't heart
At the first sight though so prevailed
        That my voice fail'd.

I'me speechless, feavrish, fires assail
My fainting flesh, my sight doth fail
Whilst to my restless mind my ears
        Still hum new fears.

Cold sweats and tremblings so invade
That like a wither'd flower I fade
So that my life being almost lost,
        I seem a Ghost.

Yet since I'me wretched must I dare.

from his translation of Longinus, 1652

THOMAS CREECH

'Young wanton Cupid's Darts and Bow'

Young wanton *Cupid*'s Darts and Bow
Have forc'd thy Spindle from thee now;
Thy wool, and all *Minerva*'s Toils
Are charming *Heber*'s Beauty's Spoils;
He lives thy Mind's continual Theme,
And you can think on nought but him.

WILLIAM BOWLES

Sapho's Ode Out of Longinus

I

The Gods are not more blest than he,
Who fixing his glad Eyes on thee,
With thy bright Rays his Senses chears,
And drinks with ever thirsty ears.
The charming Musick of thy Tongue,
Does ever hear, and ever long;
That sees with more than humane Grace,
Sweet smiles adorn thy Angel Face.

II

But when with kinder beams you shine,
And so appear much more divine,
My feeble sense and dazl'd sight,
No more support the glorious light,
And the fierce Torrent of Delight.
Oh! then I feel my Life decay,
My ravish'd Soul then flies away,
Then Faintness does my Limbs surprize,
And Darkness swims before my Eyes.

III

Then my Tongue fails, and from my Brow
The liquid drops in silence flow,
Then wand'ring Fires run through my Blood,
And Cold binds up the stupid Flood,
All pale, and breathless then I lye,
I sigh, I tremble, and I dye.

ANNE FINCH,
COUNTESS OF WINCHILSEA

Melinda on an Insipid Beauty

You, when your body life shall leave,
Must drop entire into the grave;
Unheeded, unregarded lie,
And all of you together die:
Must hide that fleeting charm, that face in dust,
Or to some painted cloth the slighted image trust;
Whilst my fam'd works shall thro' all times surprise,
My polish'd thoughts, my bright ideas rise,
And to new men be known, still talking to their eyes.

AMBROSE PHILIPS

An Hymn to Venus

I

O *Venus*, Beauty of the Skies,
To whom a thousand Temples rise,
Gayly false in gentle Smiles,
Full of Love-perplexing Wiles;
O Goddess! from my Heart remove
The wasting Cares and Pains of Love.

II

If ever thou hast kindly heard
A Song in soft Distress preferr'd,
Propitious to my tuneful Vow,
O gentle Goddess! hear me now.
Descend, thou bright, immortal Guest,
In all thy radiant Charms confest.

III

Thou once didst leave Almighty *Jove*,
And all the Golden Roofs above:
The Carr thy wanton Sparrows drew;
Hov'ring in Air they lightly flew,
As to my Bow'r they wing'd their Way:
I saw their quiv'ring Pinions play.

IV

The Birds dismist (while you remain)
Bore back their empty Carr again:
Then You, with Looks divinely mild,
In ev'ry heav'nly Feature smil'd,
And ask'd, what new Complaints I made,
And why I call'd you to my Aid?

V

What Phrenzy in my Bosom rag'd,
And by what Cure to be asswaged?
What gentle Youth I would allure,
Whom in my artful Toiles secure?
Who does thy tender Heart subdue,
Tell me, my *Sappho*, tell me Who?

VI

Tho' now he Shuns thy longing Arms,
He soon shall court thy slighted Charms:
Tho' now thy Off'rings he despise,
He soon to Thee shall Sacrifice;
Tho' now he freeze, he soon shall burn,
And be thy Victim in his turn.

VII

Celestial Visitant, once more
Thy needful Presence I implore!
In Pity come and ease my Grief,
Bring my distemper'd Soul Relief;
Favour thy Suppliant's hidden Fires,
And give me All my Heart desires.

A Fragment of Sappho

I

Bless'd as the Immortal Gods is he,
The Youth who fondly sits by thee,
And hears and sees thee all the while
Softly speak and sweetly smile.

II

Twas this depriv'd my Soul of Rest,
And rais'd such Tumults in my Breast;
For while I gaz'd, in Transport toss'd,
My Breath was gone, my Voice was lost:

III

My Bosom glow'd; the subtle Flame
Ran quick through all my vital Frame;
O'er my dim Eyes a Darkness hung;
My Ears with hollow Murmurs rung:

IV

In dewy Damps my Limbs were chill'd;
My Blood with gentle Horrours thrill'd;
My feeble Pulse forgot to play;
I fainted, sunk, and dy'd away.

JOHN ADDISON

An Hymn to Venus

Many-Scepter'd Queen of Love,
Guile-enamour'd Child of *Jove*,
Ever-honour'd! cease my Smart,
Nor oppress thy Vot'ry's Heart.

But, propitious, Oh descend!
And my tuneful Vows attend.
From thy Father's gold-roof'd Court,
Once they charm'd thy kind Resort.

Thee thy wanton Sparrows drew,
Swift on sable Wings they flew;
As they thro' the raptur'd Air,
Lightly-quiv'ring bore thy Car.

They return'd. You, Goddess, smil'd,
And with Looks divinely mild,
Ask'd, What Griefs my Peace betray'd,
Why I call'd you to my Aid.

Whence my Mind's soft Phrenzy grew?
What coy Youth I would subdue?
Whom engage in artful Toils?
Who my *Sappho*'s Heart beguiles?

Tho' thy Gifts and Thee he slight,
He shall soon with Gifts invite;
Tho' he freeze, he soon shall burn,
Thy fond Victim in his Turn.

Once again, Oh hear my Pray'r!
Loose the Bands of am'rous Care.
Present bless thy Suppliant's Fires,
Grant me all my Heart desires.

An Ode

On a YOUNG MAID whom she lov'd.

Happy as a God is he,
That fond Youth, who plac'd by thee,
Hears and sees thee sweetly gay,
Talk and smile his Soul away.

That it was alarm'd my Breast,
And depriv'd my Heart of Rest.
For in speechless Raptures tost,
Whilst I gaz'd, my Voice was lost.

The soft Fire with flowing Rein,
Glided swift thro' ev'ry Vein;
Darkness o'er my Eyelids hung;
In my Ears faint Murmurs rung.

Chilling Damps my Limbs bedew'd;
Gentle Tremors thrill'd my Blood;
Life from my pale Cheeks retir'd;
Breathless, I almost expir'd.

Fragments

I

A Fragment of SAPPHO's from Hephaestion the Grammarian

The Moon has veil'd her Silver Light,
The *Pleiades* have left the Sky;
It's now the silent Noon of Night,
The Love-sworn Hour is past; yet I
Alone, deserted, pining lie!

II

When Death shall close those Eyes, imperious Dame!
Silence shall seize on thy inglorious Name.
For thy unletter'd Hand ne'er pluck'd the Rose,
Which on *Pieria*'s happy Summit glows.
To *Pluto*'s Realms unhonour'd you shall go,
And herd amongst th'ignobler Ghosts below.
Whilst I on Wings of Fame shall rise elate,
And snatch a bright Eternity from Fate.

IV

Dire Love, sweet-bitter Bird of Prey!
    Whom nothing can controul,
Ah me! dissolves my Life away,
    And melts my inmost Soul.

The charming *Atthis*, who so late
    To *Sappho* vow'd her Care;
Now makes *Andromeda* her Fate,
    And leaves me to despair.

GEORGE JEFFREYS

An Ode from Sappho, English'd

Happy Man, the Gods excelling,
He, who close by you appears!
He who, on your Graces dwelling,
Drinks them deep at eyes and ears!

When your Words, in Music flowing,
Silent Ecstasy impart;
When your Smiles, divinely glowing,
Fire the dancing, ravish'd Heart.

In a Moment, thro' your Lover,
Warm, the soft Infection flies;
My Tongue trips, I shake all over,
Ring my Ears, and swim my Eyes.

Cold Sweat trickles; Speech forsakes me;
Blood and Sense at once retire;
Gentle Faintness overtakes me:
Now – I pant! O! now expire.

FRANCIS FAWKES

An Hymn to Venus

Venus, bright goddess of the skies,
To whom unnumber'd temples rise,
Jove's daughter fair, whose wily arts
Delude fond lovers of their hearts;
O! listen gracious to my prayer,
And free my mind from anxious care.

If e'er you heard my ardent vow,
Propitious goddess, hear me now!
And oft my ardent vow you've heard,
By Cupid's kindly aid preferr'd,
Oft left the golden courts of Jove,
To listen to my tales of love.

The radiant car your sparrows drew;
You gave the word, and swift they flew,
Through liquid air they wing'd their way,
I saw their quivering pinions play;
To my plain roof they bore their queen,
Of aspect mild, and look serene.

Soon as you came, by your command,
Back flew the wanton feather'd band,
Then, with a sweet, enchanting look,
Divinely smiling, thus you spoke:
'Why didst thou call me to thy cell?
'Tell me, my gentle Sappho, tell.

'What healing medicine shall I find
'To cure thy love distemper'd mind?
'Say, shall I lend thee all my charms,
'To win young Phaon to thy arms?
'Or does some other swain subdue
'Thy heart? my Sappho, tell me who?

'Though now, averse, thy charms he slight,
'He soon shall view thee with delight;
'Though now he scorns thy gifts to take,
'He soon to thee shall offerings make;
'Though now thy beauties fail to move,
'He soon shall melt with equal love.'

Once more, O Venus! hear my prayer,
And ease my mind of anxious care;
Again vouchsafe to be my guest,
And calm this tempest in my breast!
To thee, bright queen, my vows aspire;
O grant me all my heart's desire!

'More happy than the gods is he'

More happy than the gods is he
Who, soft-reclining, sits by thee;
His ears thy pleasing talk beguiles,
His eyes thy sweetly dimpled smiles.

This, this, alas! alarm'd my breast,
And robb'd me of my golden rest:
While gazing on thy charms I hung,
My voice died faltering on my tongue.

With subtle flames my bosom glows,
Quick through each vein the poison flows:
Dark, dimming mists my eyes surround;
My ears with hollow murmurs sound.

My limbs with dewy chillness freeze,
On my whole frame pale tremblings seize,
And losing colour, sense and breath,
I seem quite languishing in death.

Fragment i

The Pleiads now no more are seen,
Nor shines the silver moon serene,
In dark and dismal clouds o'ercast;
The Love appointed hour is past:
Midnight usurps her sable throne,
And yet, alas! I lie alone.

Fragment ii

    Whene'er the Fates resume thy breath,
        No bright reversion shalt thou gain;
    Unnotic'd shalt thou sink in death,
        Nor ev'n thy memory remain:
For thy rude hand ne'er pluck'd the lovely rose,
Which on the mountain of Pieria blows.

    To Pluto's mansions shalt thou go,
        The stern, inexorable king,
    Among th' ignoble shades below
        A vain, ignoble thing;
While honour'd Sappho's muse-embellish'd name
Shall flourish in eternity of fame.

Fragment iv

Come, gentle mother, cease your sharp reproof,
My hands no more can ply the curious woof,
While on my mind the flames of Cupid prey,
And lovely Phaon steals my soul away.

E. BURNABY GREENE

Ode 11

Happy the youth, who free from care
Is seated by the lovely Fair!
Not Gods his ecstacy can reach,
Who hears the music of thy speech;
Who views entranc'd the dimpled grace,
The smiling sweetness of thy face.

Thy smiles, thy voice with subtil art
Have rais'd the fever of my heart;
I saw Thee, and unknown to rest,
At once my senses were oppress'd;
I saw Thee, and with envy toss'd,
My voice, my very breath, was lost.

My veins a throbbing ardor prove
The transport of a jealous Love;
Ev'n in the day's meridian light
A sickly languor clouds my sight;
A hollow murmur wounds my ear,
I nothing but confusion hear.

With current cold the vital streams
Trill, slowly trill along my limbs;
Pale as the flow'ret's faded grace
An icy chillness spreads my face;
In life's last agony I lie,
– Doom'd, in a moment doom'd to die.

The Fragments of Sappho

I

The moon, with silver-gleaming eye
    Smiling a paly light,
Has pass'd, long pass'd the noon of night:
    The *Pleiades* no more
Cheer with their glimm'ring lamps the sky.
    Ah! long with envious wing has flown
        The Love appointed hour,
    While I, perfidious man, with amorous moan,
        Sink on my couch abandon'd, and alone.

II

Yet, oh! these fond complaints, dear parent, cease,
Leave me, oh! leave my wretched soul to Peace;
Think, cruel, think, – can *Sappho*'s falt'ring hand
The golden Shuttle's labor'd force command?
While glows my love-sick mind with *Cupid*'s dart,
And all the Youth comes rushing o'er my heart.

III

Love, thou sweetly-bitter pow'r,
Ruler of the human hour,
Why do'st hurl thy wanton dart
'Gainst a fond, unguarded heart?
Gentle pow'r, thy soft control
Well might melt my yielding soul,
Did my fav'rite *Atthis* prove,
(She to *Sappho* vow'd her love)
How I court the charming fair;
How she loads my breast with care!
While my rival in her mind
Rules the place to me assign'd.

WALTER SAVAGE LANDOR

'Mother, I can not mind my wheel'

Mother, I can not mind my wheel;
        My fingers ache, my lips are dry:
Oh! if you felt the pain I feel!
        But Oh, who ever felt as I?
No longer could I doubt him true . .
        All other men may use deceit;
He always said my eyes were blue,
        And often swore my lips were sweet.

GEORGE GORDON, LORD BYRON

from *Don Juan*

Oh Hesperus! thou bringest all good things –
    Home to the weary, to the hungry cheer,
To the young bird the parent's brooding wings,
    The welcome stall to the o'erlabour'd steer;
Whate'er of peace about our hearthstone clings,
    Whate'er our household gods protect of dear,
Are gather'd round us by thy look of rest;
Thou bring'st the child, too, to the mother's breast.

(CANTO 3.107)

ANON

The Loves of Sappho and Alcaeus

ALCAEUS —   I fain would speak, I fain would tell,
But shame and fear my utterance quell.
SAPPHO —   If aught of good, if aught of fair
Thy tongue were labouring to declare,
Nor shame should dash thy glance, nor fear
Forbid thy suit to reach my ear.

'Artists, raise the rafters high!'

Artists, raise the rafters high!
    Ample scope and stately plan –
Mars-like comes the bridegroom nigh,
    Loftier then a lofty man.

Edinburgh Review, 1832

DANTE GABRIEL ROSSETTI

One Girl

(A combination from Sappho)

I

Like the sweet apple which reddens upon the topmost bough,
A-top on the top-most twig, – which the pluckers forgot,
    somehow, –
Forgot it not, nay, but got it not, for none could get it till now.

II

Like the wild hyacinth flower which on the hills is found,
Which the passing feet of the shepherds for ever tear and
    wound,
Until the purple blossom is trodden into the ground.

1870 (*re-titled 'Beauty' in* 1881)

JOHN ADDINGTON SYMONDS

Hymn to Aphrodite

Star-throned incorruptible Aphrodite,
Child of Zeus, wile-weaving, I supplicate thee,
Tame not me with pangs of the heart, dread mistress,
    Nay, nor with anguish.
But come thou, if erst in the days departed
Thou didst lend thine ear to my lamentation,
And from far, the house of thy sire deserting,
    Camest with golden
Car yoked: thee thy beautiful sparrows hurried
Swift with multitudinous pinions fluttering
Round black earth, adown from the height of heaven
    Through middle ether:
Quickly journeyed they; and, O thou, blest Lady,
Smiling with those brows of undying lustre,
Asked me what new grief at my heart lay, wherefore
    Now I had called thee,
What I fain would have to assuage the torment
Of my frenzied soul; and whom now, to please thee,
Must persuasion lure to thy love, and who now,
    Sappho, hath wronged thee?
Yea, for though she flies, she shall quickly chase thee;
Yea, though gifts she spurns, she shall soon bestow them;
Yea, though now she loves not, she soon shall love thee,
    Yea, though she will not!
Come, come now too! Come, and from heavy heart-ache
Free my soul, and all that my longing yearns to
Have done, do thou; be thou for me thyself too
    Help in the battle.

'Peer of gods he seemeth...'

Peer of gods he seemeth to me, the blissful
Man who sits and gazes at thee before him,
Close beside thee sits, and in silence hears thee
    Silverly speaking,
Laughing love's low laughter. Oh this, this only
Stirs the troubled heart in my breast to tremble!
For should I but see thee a little moment,
    Straight is my voice hushed;
Yea, my tongue is broken, and through and through me
'Neath the flesh impalpable fire runs tingling;
Nothing see mine eyes, and a noise of roaring
    Waves in my ears sounds;
Sweat runs down in rivers, a tremor seizes
All my limbs, and paler than grass in autumn,
Caught by pains of menacing death, I falter,
    Lost in the love trance.

'Stars that shine ...

Stars that shine around the refulgent full moon
Pale, and hide their glory of lesser lustre
When she pours her silvery plenilunar
    Light on the orbed earth.

'Lo, Love once more...'

Lo, Love once more my soul within me rends
Like wind that on the mountain oak descends.

THOMAS HARDY

Sapphic Fragment

'Thou shalt be – Nothing.' – OMAR KHAYYÁM
'Tombless, with no remembrance.' – W. SHAKESPEARE

Dead shalt thou lie; and nought
    Be told of thee or thought,
For thou hast plucked not of the Muses' tree:
    And even in Hades' halls
    Amidst thy fellow-thralls
No friendly shade thy shade shall company!

WILLIAM ELLERY LEONARD

Full Moon

Off in the twilight hung the low full moon,
And all the women stood before it grave,
As round an altar. Thus at holy times
The Cretan damsels dance melodiously
With delicate feet about the sacrifice,
Trampling the tender bloom of the soft grass.

For Ever Dead

Death shall be death for ever unto thee,
Lady, with no remembrance of thy name
Then or thereafter; for thou gatherest not
The roses of Pieria, loving gold
Above the Muses. Even in Hades' House
Wander thou shalt unmarked, flitting forlorn
Among the shadowy, averted dead.

WILLIAM CARLOS WILLIAMS

from *Paterson,* V.II

' . I am no authority on Sappho and do not read her poetry particu-
larly well. She wrote for a clear gentle tinkling voice. She avoided all
roughness. "The silence that is in the starry sky," gives something of her
tone, . '

A.P.

Peer of the gods is that man, who
face to face, sits listening
to your sweet speech and lovely
   laughter.

It is this that rouses a tumult
in my breast. At mere sight of you
my voice falters, my tongue
   is broken.

Straightway, a delicate fire runs in
my limbs; my eyes
are blinded and my ears
   thunder.

Sweat pours out: a trembling hunts
me down. I grow paler
than dry grass and lack little
   of dying.

RICHARD ALDINGTON

To Atthis

Atthis, far from me and dear Mnasidika,
Dwells in Sardis;
Many times she was near us
So that we lived life well
Like the far-famed goddess
Whom above all things music delighted.

And now she is first among the Lydian women
As the mighty sun, the rose-fingered moon,
Beside the great stars.

And the light fades from the bitter sea
And in like manner from the rich-blossoming earth;
And the dew is shed upon the flowers,
Rose and soft meadow-sweet
And many-coloured melilote.
Many things told are remembered of sterile Atthis.

I yearn to behold thy delicate soul
To satiate my desire...

ALLEN TATE

Farewell to Anactoria

Never the tramp of foot or horse,
Nor lusty cries from ship at sea,
Shall I call loveliest on the dark earth –
       My heart moves lovingly.

I say that what one loves is best:
The midnight fastness of the heart.
Helen, you took the beauty of men
       With unpitying art!

White Paris from Idean hills
For you the Trojan towers razed –
Who swiftly ploughed the black seas
       Had on your white arm gazed!

Oh, how loving from afar
Led you to grief, for in your mind
The present was too light, as ever
       Among fair womankind....

So, Anactoria, go you away
With what calm carelessness of sorrow!
Your gleaming footstep and your grace,
       When comes another morrow,

Much would I rather then behold
Than Lydian cars or infantry.
I ask the lot of blessedness,
       Belovèd, in memory.

8   I took my lyre and said:

Come now, my heavenly
tortoise shell: become
a speaking instrument

11   We heard them chanting:

FIRST
VOICE

Young Adonis is
dying! O Cytherea
What shall we do now?

SECOND
VOICE

Batter your breasts
with your fists, girls –
tatter your dresses!

12   It's no use

Mother dear, I
can't finish my
weaving
          You may
blame Aphrodite

soft as she is

she has almost
killed me with
love for that boy

17   Sleep, darling

I have a small
daughter called
Cleis, who is

like a golden
flower
       I wouldn't
take all Croesus'
kingdom with love
thrown in, for her

37   You know the place: then

Leave Crete and come to us
waiting where the grove is
pleasantest, by precincts

sacred to you; incense
smokes on the altar, cold
streams murmur through the

apple branches, a young
rose thicket shades the ground
and quivering leaves pour

down deep sleep; in meadows
where horses have grown sleek
among spring flowers, dill

scents the air. Queen! Cyprian!
Fill our gold cups with love
stirred into clear nectar

39   He is more than a hero

He is a god in my eyes –
the man who is allowed
to sit beside you – he

who listens intimately
to the sweet murmur of
your voice, the enticing

laughter that makes my own
heart beat fast. If I meet
you suddenly, I can't

speak – my tongue is broken;
a thin flame runs under
my skin; seeing nothing,

hearing only my own ears
drumming, I drip with sweat;
trembling shakes my body

and I turn paler than
dry grass. At such times
death isn't far from me

42   I have had not one word from her

Frankly I wish I were dead.
When she left, she wept

a great deal; she said to
me, 'This parting must be
endured, Sappho. I go unwillingly.'

I said, 'Go, and be happy
but remember (you know
well) whom you leave shackled by love

'If you forget me, think
of our gifts to Aphrodite
and all the loveliness that we shared

'all the violet tiaras,
braided rosebuds, dill and
crocus twined around your young neck

'myrrh poured on your head
and on soft mats girls with
all that they most wished for beside them

'while no voices chanted
choruses without ours,
no woodlot bloomed in spring without song…'

43   It was you, Atthis, who said

'Sappho, if you will not get
up and let us look at you
I shall never love you again!

'Get up, unleash your suppleness,
lift off your Chian nightdress
and, like a lily leaning into

'a spring, bathe in the water.
Cleis is bringing your best
purple frock and the yellow

'tunic down from the clothes chest;
you will have a cloak thrown over
you and flowers crowning your hair…

'Praxinoa, my child, will you please
roast nuts for our breakfast? One
of the gods is being good to us:

'today we are going at last
into Mitylene, our favorite
city, with Sappho, loveliest

'of its women; she will walk
among us like a mother with
all her daughters around her

'when she comes home from exile...'

But you forget everything

98   It is the Muses

Who have caused me
to be honored: they
taught me their craft

RICHMOND LATTIMORE

'Some there are who say...'

Some there are who say that the fairest thing seen
on the black earth is an array of horsemen;
some, men marching; some would say ships; but I say
        she whom one loves best

is the loveliest. Light were the work to make this
plain to all, since she, who surpassed in beauty
all mortality, Helen, once forsaking
        her lordly husband,

fled away to Troy-land across the water.
Not the thought of child nor beloved parents
was remembered, after the Queen of Cyprus
        won her at first sight.

Since young brides have hearts that can be persuaded
easily, light things, palpitant to passion
as am I, remembering Anaktoria
        who has gone from me

and whose lovely walk and the shining pallor
of her face I would rather see before my
eyes than Lydia's chariots in all their glory
        armored for battle.

'When we lived all as one...'

When we lived all as one, she adored you as
symbol of some divinity,
Arignóta, delighted in your dancing.

Now she shines among Lydian women as
into dark when the sun has set
the moon, pale-handed, at last appeareth

making dim all the rest of the stars, and light
spreads afar on the deep, salt sea,
spreading likewise across the flowering cornfields;

and the dew rinses glittering from the sky;
roses spread, and the delicate
antherisk, and the lotus spreads her petals.

So she goes to and fro there, remembering
Atthis and her compassion, sick
the tender mind, and the heart with grief is eaten.

DOUGLAS YOUNG

Thon Time We Aa Wonned

Thon time we aa wonned thegither,
she was shair o ye then, and worshippt ye neist;
she loed your singan abune aa ither.

Braw amang Lydian leddies nou
she gaes, like the rose-fingert mune
wi aa the starns about her brou,

eftir the sun's doungangan. The leam
streiks out on the monie-fleurit hauchs
and kelters owre the saut sea's stream.

Doun draps the dauch in a bonnie shouer,
roses blaw rowthie, and saft chervil,
and the hinnie-sawrit clover-fleur.

Stravaigan aften her lane she'll gae,
thinkan lang til her gentie Atthis,
forfant in spreit, and her hert wae.

Til Anaktoria

Maik o the gods he seems to me,
thon man that sits in front o ye,
and hears your talkan couthilie near,
sae saftlie and clear,

your luvelie lauchan. My hert stounds
rowsan i ma breist when your lauch sounds,
and gif I glent at ye sittan there
I canna speak mair.

wonned, dwelt; *dauch*, dew; *hinnie-sawrit*, honey-smelling;
thinkan lang til, yearning for; *forfant*, faint, enfeebled

Ma tung freezes i ma mou, a nesh
lowe rins chitteran throu ma flesh;
nae sicht i ma een; wi their nain thunner
ma lugs dunner.

Swyte reems doun me; frae heid to fuit
a trummlan grups me, sae's I sit
greener nor gerss, in sic a dwalm
I kenna wha I am.

'Deid sall ye ligg…'

Deid sall ye ligg, and ne'er a memorie
sall onie hain, or ae regret for ye,
sin that ye haena roses o Pierie.
In Hades' howff a gangrel ghaist ye'll flee,
amang derk ghaists stravaigan sichtlesslie.

'Caller rain frae abune'

Caller rain frae abune
reeshles amang the epple-trees:
the leaves are soughan wi the breeze,
and sleep faas drappan doun.

'Minnie, I canna caa my wheel'

Minnie, I canna caa my wheel,
or spin the oo or twyne the tweel.
It's luve o a laddie whammles me.
Ech, the wanchancie glamarie.

---

maik, mate; *nesh*, delicate; *roses o Pierie*, the Muses' flowers; *howff*, resort
(used especially of churchyards and public houses); *minnie*, mother;
caa, drive; *oo*, wool; *tweel*, cloth; *wanchancie*, uncanny

ROBERT LOWELL

from *Three Letters to Anaktoria*

[The man or hero loves Anaktoria, later Sappho;
in the end, he withdraws or dies.]

I

I set that man above the gods and heroes –
all day, he sits before you face to face,
like a cardplayer. Your elbow brushes his elbow –
if you should speak, he hears.

The touched heart madly stirs,
your laughter is water hurrying over pebbles –
every gesture is a proclamation,
every sound is speech...

Refining fire purifies my flesh!
I hear you: a hollowness in my ears
thunders and stuns me. I cannot speak.
I cannot see.

I shiver. A dead whiteness spreads over
my body, trickling pinpricks of sweat.
I am greener than the greenest green grass –
I die!

PETER WHIGHAM

Agallíde

Equal to a god he seems who
sits listening to your sweet voice
& the sound of your Cyprian
        laughter that makes
my heart fail in my breast: I
have but to see you a little
and words die, an invisible
        flame laps at me
under my skin, I am tongue-tied,
my eyes see nothing & thunder
sounds in my ears, I sweat, shivering,
        pale as pale grass,
like a dead woman; Agallide,
it is this we must bear,
for so…

The Nightingale

The lovers' nightingale that is
the clamorous angel of the spring

Love

The wind threshes the mountain oaks.
Eros is frenzied in the soul of Sappho.

Irresistible & bitter
the mastery that sweetly melts my limbs.

The Apple

The fruit-gatherers
        have forgotten
the reddest apple
        on the tree-top,
& the sweetest.
        Forgotten?
No, not forgotten,
        left...
too high to pick –

Her Gifts

More music
                than the harp,
she yields,
                more gold
than gold...

The Moon

The stars
        that circle
her bright face
                cloak theirs
when the night-queen
                        sheds
her silver. .
        light . .
at the full

Girlhood

Like
    the wild-
flower
      where
the shepherd's
          foot
treads
    and leaves
its petalled
      print

Children's Song

Childhood, childhood where have you gone?
Will you come back to us?
Will you come back?
Ever come back?

Never come back again.
Never come back.
Never.

8

Spring
Too long
Gongyla

Is there any sign from the oracle
To the girls most of all
Hermes, at least, has entered my dreams

I said, O Lord
Not, I swear, by the blessed goddess
None can be pleased by that impending

But if ever any longed to die
To see the lotos heavy under dew
On the banks of Acheron

24

[   ]
[   ] that labor [   ]
[   ] a face to remember in wonder [
[   ]

[   ] to sing [   ]
[   ] a storm wind [   ]
[   ] and no pain [   ]
[   ]

[   ] I urge [   ]
Gongyla [   ] harp
[   ] whose longing again
Hovers on wings

Around your loveliness. For when she sees
The long pleats of your dress in their moving
She catches her breath at the beauty,
And I laugh for joy.

Goddess born from the sea at Kypros
Thus I pray [   ]
That [   ]
I long [   ].

43

[   ] Sard [is   ]
How many times she must remember us here
Where once [   ] we [   ]
She had divinity in her.

Her dancing, of all, was your enchantment.
And now she moves among the Lydian ladies
As when the sun has set and the stars come out
And the rose red moon

Lifts into the midst of their pale brightness.
Her light is everywhere, on the salt-bitter sea,
On fields thick and rich with flowers
And beautiful under dew,

On roses, tangled parsley, and the honey-headed clover.
Her light is everywhere, remembering
Atthis in her young sweetness, desiring her
With tender, heavy heart.

There, in that far place, that we come [
Knows not [   ] many
Hears [   ] the between
[   ].

They are not mine, the deerhide shoes of Asia,
That body to hold, with its goddess's beauty
To have against [
[   ].

Soft [   ] Eros
And [   ] Aphrodita
[   ] nectar poured into
Golden [   ].

[   ] enticement with her hands
[
[
                [   ].

[   ] in the month of Geraistios
[   ] lovers
[   ] never
[   ] I shall come.

78

Before my lying heart could speak for life
I longed for death. Misery the size of terror
Was in her tears when we unclasped forever.
Sappho! she cried,

That I could stay! Joy goes with you, I said,
Remember what has been, the rose and violet crowns
I wove into your hair when we stood so close together,
Heart against heart,

The garlands I plaited of flower with flower
Around your graceful neck, the oils of spices
As precious as for a queen [
[   ].

Deep in the cushions on that softest bed
Where, free in desire [
[   ] tender lovers
[   ].

None [   ] holy, and no [
There was, that we were apart from [
No sacred grove [
[   ].

101

[   ] slick with slime [   ]
[   ] Polyanaktidas to satiety [   ]
[   ] shoots forward [   ]
Playing such music upon these strings
Wearing a phallus of leather [   ]
Such a thing as this [   ] enviously
[   ] twirls quivering masterfully
[   ] and has for odor
[   ] hollow [   ]
[   ]
[   ] mysteries, orgies
[   ] leaving
[   ] an oracle
[   ] comes [   ]
[   ]
[com]panions
[mys]teries
[   ]
[   ]
[   ] sister
So [   ]
[   ] wishes [   ]
Displays again Polyanaktidas [   ]
This randy madness I joyfully proclaim.
[   ]
Her [

Man [
And see[ms
These girls al[l
Topmost [
Wanders [
[   ] these [
[   ]
Partner [
Own cousin [
Elbows [
Laughing away [
This [
The [
Cries O [
Blood [
Sharp [
[   ]
[   ]
Well [
Shall please again [
And from [
O girls [
[   ].

106

I
Stand beside me, worshipped Hera, strange in a dream,
Ghost or visitation but in a shape all grace,
Sudden as before the famous Mycenaean kings
When they cried out

At the awful end of pulling Troy to the ground,
Their ships turned homeward down the rapid Skamander,
And knew that lest you guide them they were luckless,
And prayed your love,

And called to strongest Zeus and Thyona's son
The cherished. Like them, lady queen, I ask
To return to my country, homecoming with your
Benediction,

That among the virgins of Mytilene, as before,
I perform the chaste and holy rites in splendor,
And teach the dances and make songs for the holy days.
O bring me home.

146

>] called you
>] filled your mouth with plenty
>] girls, fine gifts
>] lovesong, the keen-toned harp
>] an old woman's flesh
>] hair that used to be black
>] knees will not hold
>] stand like dappled fawns
>] but what could I do?
>] no longer able to begin again
>] rosy-armed Dawn
>] bearing to the ends of the earth
>] nevertheless seized
>] the cherished wife
>] withering is common to all
>] may that girl come and be my lover

I have loved all graceful things [   ] and this
Eros has given me, beauty and the light of the sun.

ROBERT BAGG

Sappho

Although I didn't say so then,
I want quite honestly to die.
She's gone, and there were a lot
of tears when she said, *Can you
still feel how we touched each other,
Sappho – I hate leaving you.*
Don't you see (I said) listen,
why not leave radiant
as if you remembered the
honey of it? Why make me tell you
things you can't have forgotten?
How lazy and sensual we were,
busy with headbands of violets
roses crocuses – all you bunched
in rings and piled over me,
silly necklaces full of silky
petals, slippery damp on my
soft neck. And your palms, wet with
rare royal myrrh shampoo, would
massage and rinse out my lovely hair...

DAVID CONSTANTINE

'Some say nothing on earth'

Some say nothing on earth excels in beauty
Fighting men, and call incomparable the lines
Of horse or foot or ships. Let us say rather
Best is what one loves.

This among any who have ever loved
Never wanted proof. Consider Helen: she

Whom in beauty no other woman came near
Left the finest man

In Greece and followed a much worse to Troy
Across the sea and in that city forgot
Father, mother and her baby girl. For where
Cypris led her there

She followed as women will who are all
Malleable under love and easily turned.
My absent Anaktoria do not likewise
Put me from your thoughts.

For one glimpse of your lovely walk, to see
The radiance of your face again I'd give
The chariots of all Lydia and all their
Armoured fighting men.

'Gods are not happier'

Gods are not happier than I think he
Must be who sits before you face to face
Listening closely to your every word
Beloved girl I

See how he loves to hear your laughter, my
Beloved laughing girl, it hurts my heart
When I see you I cannot speak, nothing
Comes to me to say

My tongue is tied and at the sight of you
I have the sensation of fine fire
My eyes are blinded and there is the din of
Deafness in my ears

The sweat streams down me cold, I am shaken
Through and through and look lanker than the grass
In summer. I think I cannot bear much more,
My life will fail me.

'Dead and going below...'

Dead and going below you will leave a memory
Unable to survive. For of their roses, who inhabit Pieria,
You had no share. Your soul, flying from here, in Hell
Will trail obscurely among the shadowy dead.

2

REPRESENTATIONS

MYTHS, MEDITATIONS AND TRAVESTIES

JOHN DONNE

Sappho to Philaenis

Where is that holy fire, which verse is said
    To have? is that enchanting force decayed?
Verse, that draws Nature's works, from Nature's law,
    Thee, her best work, to her work cannot draw.
Have my tears quenched my old poetic fire;
    Why quenched they not as well, that of desire?
Thoughts, my mind's creatures, often are with thee,
    But I, their maker, want their liberty.
Only thine image, in my heart, doth sit,
    But that is wax, and fires environ it.
My fires have driven, thine have drawn it hence;
    And I am robbed of picture, heart, and sense.
Dwells with me still mine irksome memory,
    Which, both to keep, and lose, grieves equally.
That tells me how fair thou art: thou art so fair,
    As, gods, when gods to thee I do compare,
Are graced thereby; and to make blind men see,
    What things gods are, I say they are like to thee.
For, if we justly call each silly man
    A little world, what shall we call thee then?
Thou art not soft, and clear, and straight, and fair,
    As down, as stars, cedars, and lilies are,
But thy right hand, and cheek, and eye, only
    Are like thy other hand, and cheek, and eye.
Such was my Phao awhile, but shall be never,
    As thou wast, art, and, oh, mayst thou be ever.
Here lovers swear in their idolatry,
    That I am such; but grief discolours me.
And yet I grieve the less, lest grief remove
    My beauty, and make me unworthy of thy love.
Plays some soft boy with thee, oh there wants yet
    A mutual feeling which should sweeten it.
His chin, a thorny hairy unevenness
    Doth threaten, and some daily change possess.

Thy body is a natural paradise,
    In whose self, unmanured, all pleasure lies,
Nor needs perfection; why shouldst thou then
    Admit the tillage of a harsh rough man?
Men leave behind them that which their sin shows,
    And are as thieves traced, which rob when it snows.
But of our dalliance no more signs there are,
    Than fishes leave in streams, or birds in air.
And between us all sweetness may be had;
    All, all that Nature yields, or Art can add.
My two lips, eyes, thighs, differ from thy two,
    But so, as thine from one another do;
And, oh, no more; the likeness being such,
    Why should they not alike in all parts touch?
Hand to strange hand, lip to lip none denies;
    Why should they breast to breast, or thighs to thighs?
Likeness begets such strange self flattery,
    That touching myself, all seems done to thee.
Myself I embrace, and mine own hands I kiss,
    And amorously thank myself for this.
Me, in my glass, I call thee; but alas,
    When I would kiss, tears dim mine eyes, and glass.
O cure this loving madness, and restore
    Me to me; thee, my half, my all, my more.
So may thy cheeks' red outwear scarlet dye,
    And their white, whiteness of the galaxy,
So may thy mighty, amazing beauty move
    Envy in all women, and in all men, love,
And so be change, and sickness, far from thee,
    As thou by coming near, keep'st them from me.

ALEXANDER RADCLIFFE

Sapho to Phaon

THE ARGUMENT

Sapho was a Lady very Eminent for Singing of Ballads, and upon an
extraordinary Pinch, could make One well enough for her Purpose:
She held a League with one *Phaon*, who was her Companion and
Partner in the *Chorus*; but Phaon deserted his Consort for the
Preferment of a Rubber in the *ba'nnio*. *Sapho* took this so to heart, that
she threatens to break her Neck out of a Garret Window; which, if
effected, might prove her utter Destruction. Authors have not agreed
concerning the execution of her Design. But however she Writes him
this loving and terrifying Epistle.

When these my doggrel Rhimes you chance to see,
You hardly will believe they came from me,
Till you discover *Sapho*'s Name at bottom,
You'l not imagine who it is that wrote 'em:
I, that have often Sung – *Young* Phaon *strove*,
Now Sing this doleful Tune – *Farewel my Love*;
I must not Sing new Jiggs – the more's the Pity,
But must take up with some old Mournful Ditty.
You in the *Bannio* have a Place, I hear;
I in my Garret Sweat as much, with Fear;
You can rub out a Living well enough,
My Rent's unpaid, poor *Sapho* must rub off;
My Voice is crack't, and now I only houl,
And cannot hit a Treble for my Soul:
My Ballads lye neglected on a Shelf,
I cannot bear the Burthen by my self;
Doll Price the Hawker offers very fair,
She'l Sing along with me for Quarter-share;
Sue Smith, the very same will undertake,
Their Voice is like the winding of a Jack.
Hang 'em, I long to bear a Part with you,
I love to Sing, and look upon you too;

Besides, you know when Songs grow out of fashion,
That I can make a Ballad on occasion.
I am not very Beautiful, – God knows;
Yet you should value one that can Compose;
Despise me not, though I'm a little Dowdy,
I can do that – same – like a bigger Body:
Perhaps you'l say, I've but a tawny Skin;
What then? you know my Metal's good within.
What if my Shoulder's higher than my Head?
I've heard you say, I'm Shape enough a-Bed:
The Mayor (God bless him) or the worthy Sheriffs
Do very often meet with homely Wives.
Our Master too; that little scrubbed Draper,
Has he not got a Lady that's a Strapper?
If you will have a Beauty, or have none,
Phaon must lye – *Phaon* must lye alone:
I can remember, 'fore my Voice was broke,
How much in praise of me you often spoke,
And when I shook a Trill, you shook your Ears,
And swore I Sung like, what d'ee call 'em – Spheres;
You kiss'd me hard, and call'd me Charming witch,
I can't do't now, if you wou'd kiss my Breech.
Then you not only lik'd my airy Voice,
But in my Fleshly part you did Rejoice;
And when you clasp'd me in your brawny clutches,
You swore I mov'd my Body like a Dutchess;
You clap'd my Buttocks, o're and o're agen,
I can't believe that I was crooked then.
Beware of him, you Sisters of the quill,
That sing at *Smithfield-Bars*, or *Saffron-Hill*,
Who, for an honest Living, tear your Throat;
If *Phaon* drinks w'ye, you're not worth a groat:
And Ladies know, 'twill be a very hard thing
To sink from him the smallest Copper-farthing;
Avoid him all – for he has us'd me so,
Wou'd make your hearts ake, if you did but know.
My Hair's about my Ears, as I'm a Sinner,
He has not left me worth a Hood or Pinner.
Phaon by me unworthily has dealt,
Has got my Ring, – though 'twas but Copper gilt;

Yet that which vexes me, – Th' ungrateful Pimp
Has stole away my Petticoat with Gimp;
Has all my Things, but had he left me any
I can't go out alone, to get a Penny.
Phaon, I should have had less cause to grieve,
If like a Man of Sense, you'd taken leave:
That you'd be gone, had I been ne'r so certain,
We might have drank a Pot or two at parting;
Or fry'd some Bacon with an Egg; or if
Into some Steaks, we'd cut a pound of Beif,
And laugh'd awhile, that had been somthing like;
But to steal off, was but a sneaking Trick.
My Landlady can tell, how I was troubled,
When I perceiv'd my self so plainly bubbled:
I ran like mad out at the Alley-Gate
To overtake you, but it was too late:
When I consider'd I had lost my Coat,
If I had had a Knife, I'd cut my Throat;
Yet notwithstanding all the ills you did,
I Dream of you as soon as I'm in Bed;
You tickle me, and cry, Do'st like it *Saff?*
Oh wondrous well! and then methinks I laugh.
Sometimes we mingle Legs, and Arms, and Thighs,
Something between the sheets, methinks does rise:
But when I wake, and find my Dream's in vain,
I turn to sleep, only to Dream again.
When I am up, I walk about my Garret
And talk I know not what – just like a Parrot:
I move about the Room from Bed to Chair,
And have no Satisfaction any where.
The last time I remember you lay here,
We both were dry ith' Night, and went for Beer:
Into the Cellar by good luck we got,
What we did there, I'm sure you ha'n't forgot:
There stands, you know, an antiquated Tub,
'Gainst which, since that, I often stand, and rub;
Only to see't, as much delight I take
As if the Vessel now were full of Sack;
But more to add unto my Discontent,
There's been no Drink ith' Cellar since you went.

There's nothing but affords me Misery,
My Linnet in the Cage, I fear will dye:
The Bird is just like me in every thing;
Like me it pines, like me it cannot Sing.
Now *Phaon*, Pray take notice what I say,
If you don't bring the things you took away;
You know, my Garret is four Stories high;
From thence I'll leap, and in the Streets I'll die:
May be you will refuse to come – Do – do,
Y'had best let *Sapho* break her Neck for you.

Your afflicted Consort, Sapho.

from *Ovid's travestie: a burlesque upon Ovid's 'Epistles'*, 1681

NICHOLAS ROWE

Song

While *Sappho*, with harmonious airs,
Her dear *Philenis* charms,
With equal joy the nymph appears,
Dissolving in her arms.

Thus to themselves alone they are,
What all Mankind can give;
Alternately the happy pair
All grant, and all receive.

Like the twin-stars, so fam'd for friends,
Who set by turns, and rise;
When one to *Thetis*' lap descends,
His brother mounts the skies.

With happier fate, and kinder care,
These nymphs by turns do reign,
While still the falling, does prepare
The rising, to sustain

The joys of either sex in love,
In each of them we read,
Successive each, to each does prove,
Fierce youth and yielding maid.

from *Tractatus de Hermaphroditis: or, a Treatise of Hermaphrodites*
by Giles Jacob, 1718

ALEXANDER POPE

from *Sapho to Phaon*

(OVID, *Heroides* XV)

Say, lovely Youth, that dost my Heart command,
Can *Phaon*'s Eyes forget his *Sapho*'s Hand?
Must then her Name the wretched Writer prove?
To thy Remembrance lost, as to thy Love!
Ask not the cause that I new Numbers chuse,
The Lute neglected, and the Lyric Muse;
Love taught my Tears in sadder Notes to flow,
And tun'd my Heart to Elegies of Woe.
I burn, I burn, as when thro' ripen'd Corn
By driving Winds the spreading Flames are born!
Phaon to *Aetna*'s scorching Fields retires,
While I consume with more than *Aetna*'s Fires!
No more my Soul a Charm in Musick finds,
Musick has Charms alone for peaceful Minds:
Soft Scenes of Solitude no more can please,
Love enters there, and I'm my own Disease:
No more the *Lesbian* Dames my Passion move,
Once the dear Objects of my guilty Love;
All other Loves are lost in only thine,
Ah Youth ungrateful to a Flame like mine!
Whom wou'd not all those blooming Charms surprize,
Those heav'nly Looks, and dear deluding Eyes?
The Harp and Bow wou'd you like *Phoebus bear*,
A brighter *Phoebus*, *Phaon* might appear;
Wou'd you with Ivy wreath your flowing Hair,
Not *Bacchus*' self with *Phaon* cou'd compare:
Yet *Phoebus* lov'd, and *Bacchus* felt the Flame,
One *Daphne* warm'd, and one the *Cretan* Dame;
Nymphs that in Verse no more cou'd rival me,
Than ev'n those Gods contend in Charms with thee.
The Muses teach me all their softest Lays,
And the wide World resounds with *Sapho*'s Praise.
Tho' great *Alcaeus* more sublimely sings,

And strikes with bolder Rage the sounding Strings,
No less Renown attends the moving Lyre,
Which *Venus* tunes, and all her Loves inspire.
To me what Nature has in Charms deny'd
Is well by Wit's more lasting Flames supply'd.
Tho' short my Stature, yet my Name extends
To Heav'n it self, and Earth's remotest Ends.

★ ★ ★

See, while I write, my Words are lost in Tears;
The less my Sense, the more my Love appears.
Sure 'twas not much to bid one kind Adieu,
(At least to feign was never hard to you.)
Farewel my Lesbian *Love*! you might have said,
Or coldly thus, *Farewel* oh Lesbian *Maid*!
No Tear did you, no parting Kiss receive,
Nor knew I then how much I was to grieve.
No Lover's Gift your *Sapho* cou'd confer,
And Wrongs and Woes were all you left with her.
No Charge I gave you, and no Charge cou'd give,
But this; *Be mindful of our Loves, and live.*
Now by the Nine, those Pow'rs ador'd by me,
And Love, the God that ever waits on thee,
When first I heard (from whom I hardly knew)
That you were fled, and all my Joys with you,
Like some sad Statue, speechless, pale, I stood;
Grief chill'd my Breast, and stop'd my freezing Blood;
No Sigh to rise, no Tear had pow'r to flow;
Fix'd in a stupid Lethargy of Woe.
But when its way th'impetuous Passion found,
I rend my Tresses, and my Breast I wound,
I rave, then weep, I curse, and then complain,
Now swell to Rage, now melt in Tears again.
Not fiercer Pangs distract the mournful Dame,
Whose first-born Infant feeds the Fun'ral Flame.
My scornful Brother with a Smile appears,
Insults my Woes, and triumphs in my Tears,
His hated Image ever haunts my Eyes,
And *why this Grief? thy Daughter lives*; he cries.
Stung with my Love, and furious with Despair,

All torn my Garments, and my Bosom bare,
My Woes, thy Crimes, I to the World proclaim;
Such inconsistent things are Love and Shame!

'Tis thou art all my Care and my Delight,
My daily Longing, and my Dream by Night:
O Night more pleasing than the brightest Day,
When Fancy gives what Absence takes away,
And drest in all its visionary Charms,
Restores my fair Deserter to my Arms!
Then round your Neck in wanton Wreaths I twine,
Then you, methinks, as fondly circle mine:
A thousand tender Words, I hear and speak;
A thousand melting Kisses, give, and take:
Then fiercer Joys – I blush to mention these,
Yet while I blush, confess how much they please!
But when with Day the sweet Delusions fly,
And all things wake to Life and Joy, but I,
As if once more forsaken, I complain,
And close my Eyes, to dream of you again.
Then frantick rise, and like some Fury rove
Thro' lonely Plains, and thro' the silent Grove,
As if the silent Grove, and lonely Plains
That knew my Pleasures, cou'd relieve my Pains.
I view the *Grotto*, once the Scene of Love,
The Rocks around, the hanging Roofs above,
That charm'd me more, with Native Moss o'ergrown,
Than *Phrygian* Marble or the *Parian* Stone.
I find the Shades that veil'd our Joys before,
But, *Phaon* gone, those Shades delight no more.
Here the prest Herbs with bending Tops betray
Where oft entwin'd in am'rous Folds we lay;
I kiss that Earth which once was prest by you,
And all with Tears the with'ring Herbs bedew.
For thee the fading Trees appear to mourn,
And Birds defer their Songs till thy Return:
Night shades the Groves, and all in Silence lye,
All, but the mournful *Philomel* and I:
With mournful *Philomel* I join my Strain,
Of *Tereus* she, of *Phaon* I complain.

★ ★ ★

Alas! the Muses now no more inspire,
Untun'd my Lute, and silent is my Lyre,
My languid Numbers have forgot to flow,
And Fancy sinks beneath a Weight of Woe.
Ye *Lesbian* Virgins, and ye *Lesbian* Dames,
Themes of my Verse, and Objects of my Flames,
No more your Groves with my glad Songs shall ring,
No more these Hands shall touch the trembling String:
My *Phaon*'s fled, and I those Arts resign,
(Wretch that I am, to call that *Phaon* mine!)
Return fair Youth, return, and bring along
Joy to my Soul, and Vigour to my Song:
Absent from thee, the Poet's Flame expires,
But ah! how fiercely burn the Lover's Fires?
Gods! can no Pray'rs, no Sighs, no Numbers move
One savage Heart, or teach it how to love?
The Winds my Pray'rs, my Sighs, my Numbers bear
The flying Winds have lost them all in Air!
Oh when, alas! shall more auspicious Gales
To these fond Eyes restore thy welcome Sails?
If you return – ah why these long Delays?
Poor *Sapho* dies while careless *Phaon* stays.
O launch thy Bark, nor fear the watry Plain,
Venus for thee shall smooth her native Main.
O launch thy Bark, secure of prosp'rous Gales,
Cupid for thee shall spread the swelling Sails.
If you will fly – (yet ah! what Cause can be,
Too cruel Youth, that you shou'd fly from me?)
If not from *Phaon* I must hope for Ease,
Ah let me seek it from the raging Seas:
To raging Seas unpity'd I'll remove,
And either cease to live, or cease to love!

[lines 1–40, 109–78, 228–end]

MARK AKENSIDE

from *Ode* XIII. *On Lyric Poetry*

Broke from the fetters of his native land,
   Devoting shame and vengeance to her lords,
With louder impulse and a threatening hand
    The Lesbian patriot★ smiles the sounding chords:
      Ye wretches, ye perfidious train,
      Ye cursed of gods and free-born men,
        Ye murderers of the laws,
     Though now ye glory in your lust,
    Though now ye tread the feeble neck in dust,
Yet Time and righteous Jove will judge your dreadful cause.

But lo, to Sappho's melting airs
   Descends the radiant queen of Love:
She smiles, and asks what fonder cares
   Her suppliant's plaintive measures move:
Why is my faithful maid distressed?
Who, Sappho, wounds thy tender breast?
   Say, flies he? – Soon he shall pursue:
Shuns he thy gifts? – He soon shall give:
Slights he thy sorrows? – He shall grieve,
   And soon to all thy wishes bow.

★ Alkaios

96

TOBIAS SMOLLETT

from *The Adventures of Roderick Random*

Thy fatal shafts unerring move,
I bow before thine altar, Love.
I feel thy soft resistless flame
Glide swift through all my vital frame.

For while I gaze my bosom glows,
My blood in tides impetuous flows,
Hope, fear, and joy alternate roll,
And floods of transports whelm my soul.

My faltering tongue attempts in vain
In soothing murmurs to complain;
Thy tongue some secret magic ties,
Thy murmurs sink in broken sighs.

Condemned to nurse eternal care,
And ever drop the silent tear,
Unheard I mourn, unknown I sigh,
Unfriended live, unpitied die.

ELIZABETH MOODY

Sappho Burns her Books and Cultivates the Culinary Arts

[On Miss R.P.'s Saying she would find Love only if she did so]

Companions of my favourite hours,
By winter's fire, in summer's bowers,
That wont to chase my bosom's care,
And plant your pleasing visions there!
Guarini, Dante, honoured names,
Ah, doomed to feel devouring flames!
Alas, my Petrarch's gentle loves!
My Tasso's rich enchanted groves!
My Ariosto's fairy dreams,
And all my loved Italian themes!
I saw you on the pile expire,
Weeping I saw the invading fire;
There fixed remained my aching sight,
Till the last ray of parting light
The last pale flame consumed away,
And all dissolved your relics lay.

    Goddess of Culinary Art,
Now take possession of my heart!
Teach me more winning arts to try,
To salt the ham, to mix the pie;
To make the paste both light and thin,
To smooth it with the rolling-pin;
With taper skewer to print it round,
Lest ruder touch the surface wound.
Then teach thy votary how to make
That fair rotundo – a plum-cake;
To shake the compound sweets together,
To bake it light as any feather,
That, when complete, its form may show
A rising hillock topped with snow;

And how to make the cheesecake, say
To beat the eggs and turn the whey;
To strain my jelly fair and clear,
That here no *misty fog* appear;
But plain to view each form may rise
That in its glassy bosom lies.

Now fancy soars to future times,
When all extinct are Sappho's rhymes;
When none but cooks applaud her name,
And naught but recipes her fame.
When sweetest numbers she'll despise,
When Pope shall sing beneath *minced-pies*,
And Eloise in her *tin* shall mourn
Disastrous fate and love forlorn;
Achilles too, that godlike man,
Shall bluster in the *patty-pan*;
And many a once-loved Grecian chief
Shall guard from flames the roasting beef.

Then, when this transformation's made,
And Sappho's vestments speak her trade;
When girt in towels she is seen,
With cuffs to keep the elbows clean:
Then, Sorceress, she'll call on thee!
Accomplish then thy fair decree!
If, like your sisters of the heath,
Whose mystic sound betrayed Macbeth,
Fallacious charms your arts dispense,
To cheat her with ambiguous sense;
Severest torments may you prove! –
Severest – disappointed love.

GEORGE DYER

Ode XXVI. *The Resolve*

SUPPOSED TO BE WRITTEN BY SAPPHO

Yes, I have loved: yet often have I said,
Love in this breast shall never revel more;
But I will listen to wild ocean's roar,
Or, like some out-cast solitary shade,
Will cling upon the howlings of the wind,
Till I grow deaf with listening, cold and blind.
But, ah! enchantress, cease that tender lay,
Nor tune that lyre to notes thus softly slow;
Those eyes, oh take those melting eyes away!
Nor let those lips with honey'd sweets o'erflow,
Nor let meek Pity pale that lovely cheek,
Nor weep, as wretches their long sufferings speak:
With forms so fair endued, oh! Venus, why
Are Lesbian maids, or with such weakness I?
Do Lesbian damsels touch the melting lyre?
My lyre is mute; and I in silence gaze;
As tho' the muse did not this breast inspire,
I lose, in tenderer loves, the love of praise.
Oh! Sappho, how art thou imprisoned round,
Beauty's weak captive, fast-enchained with sound!
Frail, frail resolve! vain promise of a day!
I see, I hear, I feel, and melt away.

MARY ROBINSON

from *Sappho and Phaon*

Sonnet XXI

Why do I live to loath the cheerful day,
    To shun the smiles of Fame, and mark the hours
    On tardy pinions move, while ceaseless show'rs
Down my wan cheek in lucid currents stray?
My tresses all unbound, nor gems display,
    Nor scents Arabian! on my path no flow'rs
    Imbibe the morn's resuscitating pow'rs,
For one blank sorrow, saddens all my way!
    As slow the radiant Sun of reason rose,
Through tears my dying parents saw it shine;
    A brother's frailties, swell'd the tide of woes, –
And, keener far, maternal griefs were mine!
    Phaon! if soon these weary eyes shall close,
Oh! must that task, that mournful task, be thine?

Sonnet XXXIII

I wake! delusive phantoms hence, away!
    Tempt not the weakness of a lover's breast;
    The softest breeze can shake the halcyon's nest,
And lightest clouds o'ercast the dawning ray!
'Twas but a vision! Now, the star of day
    Peers, like a gem on Aetna's burning crest!
    Wellcome, ye Hills, with golden vintage drest;
Sicilian forests brown, and vallies gay!
    A mournful stranger, from the Lesbian Isle,
Not strange, in loftiest eulogy of Song!
    She, who could teach the Stoic's cheek to smile,
Thaw the cold heart, and chain the wond'ring throng,
    Can find no balm, love's sorrows to beguile;
Ah! Sorrows known too soon! and felt too long!

Sonnet XXXVI

Lead me, Sicilian Maids, to haunted bow'rs,
    While yon pale moon displays her faintest beams
    O'er blasted woodlands, and enchanted streams,
Whose banks infect the breeze with pois'nous flow'rs.
Ah! lead me, where the barren mountain tow'rs,
    Where no sounds echo, but the night-owl's screams,
    Where some lone spirit of the desart gleams,
And lurid horrors wing the fateful hours!
    Now goaded frenzy grasps my shrinking brain,
Her touch absorbs the crystal fount of woe!
    My blood rolls burning through each gasping vein;
Away, lost Lyre! unless thou can'st bestow
    A charm, to lull that agonizing pain,
Which those who never lov'd, can never know!

Sonnet XLIV. Conclusive.

Here droops the muse! while from her glowing mind,
    Celestial Sympathy, with humid eye,
    Bids the light Sylph capricious Fancy fly,
Time's restless wings with transient flow'rs to bind!
For now, with folded arms and head inclin'd,
    Reflection pours the deep and frequent sigh,
    O'er the dark scroll of human destiny,
Where gaudy buds and wounding thorns are twin'd.
    O! Sky-born VIRTUE! sacred is thy name!
And though mysterious Fate, with frown severe,
    Oft decorates thy brows with wreaths of Fame,
Bespangled o'er with sorrow's chilling tear!
    Yet shalt thou more than mortal raptures claim,
The brightest planet of th' ETERNAL SPHERE!

SAMUEL TAYLOR COLERIDGE

Alcaeus to Sappho

How sweet, when crimson colours dart
Across a breast of snow,
To see that you are in the heart
That beats and throbs below.

All Heaven is in a maiden's blush,
In which the soul doth speak,
That it was you who sent the flush
Into the maiden's cheek.

Large steadfast eyes! eyes gently rolled
In shades of changing blue,
How sweet are they, if they behold
No dearer sight than you.

And, can a lip more richly glow,
Or be more fair than this?
The world will surely answer, No!
I, Sappho, answer, Yes!

Then grant one smile, tho' it should mean
A thing of doubtful birth;
That I may say these eyes have seen
The fairest face on earth!

WALTER SAVAGE LANDOR

from *Pericles and Aspasia*

from XLVII: CLEONE TO ASPASIA

I will not interfere any farther with your reflections; and indeed
when I began, I intended to remark only the injustice of
Sappho's reproof to Alcaeus in the first instance, and the justice
of it in the second, when he renewed his suit to her after he had
fled from battle. We find it in the only epigram attributed to her.

> He who from battle runs away
> May pray and sing, and sing and pray;
> Nathless, Alcaeus, howsoe'er
> Dulcet his song and warm his prayer
> And true his vows of love may be,
> He ne'er shall run away with me.

from CXLIX: ASPASIA TO CLEONE

Among the poems of Sappho I find the following, but written in
a different hand from the rest. It pleases me at least as much as
any of them; if it is worse, I wish you would tell me in what it is
so. How many thoughts might she have turned over and tossed
away for it! Odious is the economy in preserving all the scraps of
the intellect, and troublesome the idleness of tacking them
together. Sappho is fond of seizing, as she runs on, the most
prominent and inviting flowers: she never stops to cut and trim
them: she throws twenty aside for one that she fixes in her
bosom; and what is more singular, her pleasure at their beauty
seems never to arise from another's admiration of it. See it or not
see it, there it is.

> Sweet girls! upon whose breast that God descends
>   Whom first ye pray to come, and next to spare,
> O tell me whither now his course he bends,
>   Tell me what hymn shall thither waft my prayer!

Alas! my voice and lyre alike he flies,
And only in my dreams, nor kindly then, replies.

from CL: CLEONE TO ASPASIA

Sappho to Hesperus

I have beheld thee in the morning hour
    A solitary star, with thankless eyes,
    Ungrateful as I am! who bade thee rise
When sleep all night had wandered from my bower.

    Can it be true that thou art he
    Who shinest now above the sea
Amid a thousand, but more bright?
    Ah yes, the very same art thou
    That heard me then, and hearest now . .
Thou seemest, star of love! to throb with light.

Sappho's Expostulation

Forget thee? when? *Thou* biddest me? dost *thou*
Bid me, what men alone can, break my vow?
O my too well beloved! is there aught
I ever have forgot which thou hast taught?
And shall the lesson first by thee imprest
Drop, chapter after chapter, from my breast?
Since love's last flickering flame from thine is gone,
Leave me, O leave me stil, at least my own.
Let it burn on, if only to consume,
And light me, tho it light me to the tomb.
    False are our dreams or there are fields below
To which the weariest feet the swiftest go;
And there are bitter streams the wretched bless,
Before whose thirst they lose their bitterness.
'Tis hard to love! to unlove harder yet!
Not so to die . . and then . . perhaps . . forget.

THOMAS MOORE

from *Evenings in Greece*: SONG

As o'er her loom the Lesbian Maid
    In love-sick languor hung her head,
Unknowing where her fingers stray'd,
    She weeping turn'd away, and said
'Oh, my sweet Mother – 'tis in vain –
    I cannot weave, as once I wove –
So wilder'd is my heart and brain
    With thinking of that youth I love!'

Again the web she tried to trace,
    But tears fell o'er each tangled thread;
While, looking in her mother's face,
    Who watchful o'er her lean'd, she said
'Oh, my sweet Mother – 'tis in vain –
    I cannot weave, as once I wove –
So wilder'd is my heart and brain
    With thinking of that youth I love!'

FELICIA HEMANS

The Last Song of Sappho

Suggested by a beautiful sketch, the design of the younger Westmacott. It represents Sappho sitting on a rock above the sea, with her lyre cast at her feet. There is a desolate grace about the whole figure, which seems penetrated with the feeling of utter abandonment.

Sound on, thou dark unslumbering sea!
My dirge is in thy moan;
My spirit finds response in thee,
To its own ceaseless cry – 'Alone, alone!'

Yet send me back one other word,
Ye tones that never cease!
Oh! let your secret caves be stirr'd,
And say, dark waters! will ye give me peace?

Away! my weary soul hath sought
In vain one echoing sigh,
One answer to consuming thought
In human hearts – and will the wave reply?

Sound on, thou dark unslumbering sea!
Sound in thy scorn and pride!
I ask not, alien world, from thee,
What my own kindred earth hath still denied.

And yet I loved that earth so well,
With all its lovely things!
– Was it for this the death-wind fell
On my rich lyre, and quench'd its living strings?

– Let them lie silent at my feet!
Since broken even as they,
The heart whose music made them sweet,
Hath pour'd on desert-sands its wealth away,

Yet glory's light hath touch'd my name,
The laurel-wreath is mine –
– With a lone heart, a weary frame –
O restless deep! I come to make them thine!

Give to that crown, that burning crown,
Place in thy darkest hold!
Bury my anguish, my renown,
With hidden wrecks, lost gems, and wasted gold.

Thou sea-bird on the billow's crest,
Thou hast thy love, thy home;
They wait thee in the quiet nest,
And I, th' unsought, unwatch'd-for – I too come!

I, with this winged nature fraught,
These visions wildly free,
This boundless love, this fiery thought –
– Alone I come – oh! give me peace, dark sea!

L.E.L.

Sappho's Song

Farewell, my lute! – and would that I
    Had never waked thy burning chords!
Poison has been upon thy sigh,
    And fever has breathed in thy words.

Yet wherefore, wherefore should I blame
    Thy power, thy spell, my gentlest lute?
I should have been the wretch I am,
    Had every chord of thine been mute.

It was my evil star above,
    Not my sweet lute, that wrought me wrong;
It was not song that taught me love,
    But it was love that taught me song.

If song be past, and hope undone,
    And pulse, and head, and heart, are flame;
It is thy work, thou faithless one!
    But, no! – I will not name thy name!

Sun-god! lute, wreath are vowed to thee!
    Long be their light upon my grave –
My glorious grave – you deep blue sea
    I shall sleep calm beneath its wave!

from *The Improvisatrice*

CAROLINE NORTON

The Picture of Sappho

Thou! whose impassion'd face
The Painter loves to trace,
Theme of the Sculptor's art and Poet's story –
How many a wand'ring thought
Thy loveliness hath brought,
Warming the heart with its imagined glory!

Yet, was it History's truth,
That tale of wasted youth,
Of endless grief, and Love forsaken pining?
What wert thou, thou whose woe
The old traditions show
With Fame's cold light around thee vainly shining?

Didst thou indeed sit there
In languid lone despair –
Thy harp neglected by thee idly lying –
Thy soft and earnest gaze
Watching the lingering rays
In the far west, where summer-day was dying –

While with low rustling wings,
Among the quivering strings
The murmuring breeze faint melody was making,
As though it wooed thy hand
To strike with new command,
Or mourn'd with thee because thy heart was breaking?

Didst thou, as day by day
Roll'd heavily away,
And left thee anxious, nerveless, and dejected,
Wandering thro' bowers beloved –
Roving where *he* had roved –
Yearn for his presence, as for one expected?

Didst thou, with fond wild eyes
Fix'd on the starry skies,
Wait feverishly for each new day to waken –
Trusting some glorious morn
Might witness his return,
Unwilling to believe thyself forsaken?

And when conviction came,
Chilling that heart of flame,
Didst thou, O saddest of earth's grieving daughters!
From the Leucadian steep
Dash, with a desperate leap,
And hide thyself within the whelming waters?

Yea, in their hollow breast
Thy heart at length found rest!
The ever-moving waves above thee closing –
The winds, whose ruffling sigh
Swept the blue waters by,
Disturb'd thee not! – thou wert in peace reposing!

Such is the tale they tell!
Vain was thy beauty's spell –
Vain all the praise thy song could still inspire –
Though many a happy band
Rung with less skilful hand
The borrowed love-notes of thy echoing lyre.

FAME, to thy breaking heart
No comfort could impart,
In vain thy brow the laurel wreath was wearing;
One grief and one alone
Could bow thy bright head down –
Thou wert a WOMAN, and wert left despairing!

ALFRED, LORD TENNYSON

from *Eleänore*

VIII
But when I see thee roam, with tresses unconfined,
While the amorous, odorous wind
   Breathes low between the sunset and the moon;
    Or, in a shadowy saloon,
On silken cushions half reclined;
     I watch thy grace; and in its place
     My heart a charmed slumber keeps,
      While I muse upon thy face;
      And a languid fire creeps
       Thro' my veins to all my frame,
   Dissolvingly and slowly: soon
     From thy rose-red lips MY name
Floweth; and then, as in a swoon,
    With dinning sound my ears are rife,
     My tremulous tongue faltereth,
     I lose my colour, I lose my breath,
     I drink the cup of a costly death,
Brimm'd with delirious draughts of warmest life.
     I die with my delight, before
       I hear what I would hear from thee;
       Yet tell my name again to me,
     I *would* be dying evermore,
     So dying ever, Eleänore.

CHRISTINA ROSSETTI

Sappho

I sigh at day-dawn, and I sigh
When the dull day is passing by.
I sigh at evening, and again
I sigh when night brings sleep to men.
Oh! it were better far to die
Than thus for ever mourn and sigh,
And in death's dreamless sleep to be
Unconscious that none weep for me;
Eased from my weight of heaviness,
Forgetful of forgetfulness,
Resting from pain and care and sorrow
Thro' the long night that knows no morrow;
Living unloved, to die unknown,
Unwept, untended and alone.

What Sappho would have said had her leap cured instead of killing her.

Love, Love, that having found a heart
    And left it, leav'st it desolate; –
    Love, Love, that art more strong than Hate,
More lasting and more full of art; –
O blessèd Love, return, return,
Brighten the flame that needs must burn.

Among the stately lilies pale,
    Among the roses flushing red,
    I seek a flower meet for my head,
A wreath wherewith to bind my veil:
I seek in vain; a shadow-pain
Lies on my heart; and all in vain.

The rose hath too much life in it;
    The lily is too much at rest.
    Surely a blighted rose were best,
Or cankered lily flower more fit;
Or purple violet, withering
While yet the year is in its spring.

I walk down by the river side
    Where the low willows touch the stream;
    Beneath the ripple and sun-gleam
The slippery cold fishes glide,
Where flags and reeds and rushes lave
Their roots in the unsullied wave.

Methinks this is a drowsy place:
    Disturb me not; I fain would sleep:
    The very winds and waters keep
Their voices under; and the race
Of Time seems to stand still, for here
Is night or twilight all the year.

A very holy hushedness
    Broods here for ever: like a dove
    That, having built its nest above
A quiet place, feels the excess
Of calm sufficient, and would fain
Not wake, but drowse on without pain.

And slumbering on its mossy nest
    Haply hath dreams of pleasant Spring;
    And in its vision prunes its wing
And takes swift flight, yet is at rest.
Yea, is at rest: and still the calm
Is wrapped around it like a charm.

I would have quiet too in truth,
    And here will sojourn for a while.
    Lo; I have wandered many a mile,
Till I am foot-sore in my youth.
I will lie down; and quite forget
The doubts and fears that haunt me yet.

My pillow underneath my head
    Shall be green grass; thick fragrant leaves
    My canopy; the spider weaves
Meet curtains for my narrow bed;
And the dew can but cool my brow
That is so dry and burning now.

Ah, would that it could reach my heart,
    And fill the void that is so dry
    And aches and aches; – but what am I
To shrink from my self-purchased part?
It is in vain; is all in vain;
I must go forth and bear my pain.

Must bear my pain, till Love shall turn
    To me in pity and come back.
    His footsteps left a smouldering track
When he went forth, that still doth burn.
Oh come again, thou pain divine,
Fill me and make me wholly thine.

ALGERNON CHARLES SWINBURNE

Sapphics

All the night sleep came not upon my eyelids,
Shed not dew, nor shook nor unclosed a feather,
Yet with lips shut close and with eyes of iron
    Stood and beheld me.

Then to me so lying awake a vision
Came without sleep over the seas and touched me,
Softly touched mine eyelids and lips; and I too,
    Full of the vision,

Saw the white implacable Aphrodite,
Saw the hair unbound and the feet unsandalled
Shine as fire of sunset on western waters;
    Saw the reluctant

Feet, the straining plumes of the doves that drew
Looking always, looking with necks reverted,
Back to Lesbos, back to the hills whereunder
    Shone Mitylene;

Heard the flying feet of the Loves behind her
Make a sudden thunder upon the waters,
As the thunder flung from the strong unclosing
    Wings of a great wind.

So the goddess fled from her place, with awful
Sound of feet and thunder of wings around her;
While behind a clamour of singing women
    Severed the twilight.

Ah the singing, ah the delight, the passion!
All the Loves wept, listening; sick with anguish,
Stood the crowned nine Muses about Apollo;
    Fear was upon them,

While the tenth sang wonderful things they knew not.
Ah the tenth, the Lesbian! the nine were silent,
None endured the sound of her song for weeping;
    Laurel by laurel,

Faded all their crowns; but about her forehead,
Round her woven tresses and ashen temples
White as dead snow, paler than grass in summer,
    Ravaged with kisses,

Shone a light of fire as a crown for ever.
Yea, almost the implacable Aphrodite
Paused, and almost wept; such a song was that song,
    Yea, by her name too

Called her, saying, 'Turn to me, O my Sappho;'
Yet she turned her face from the Loves, she saw not
Tears for laughter darken immortal eyelids,
    Heard not about her

Fearful fitful wings of the doves departing,
Saw not how the bosom of Aphrodite
Shook with weeping, saw not her shaken raiment,
    Saw not her hands wrung;

Saw the Lesbians kissing across their smitten
Lutes with lips more sweet than the sound of lute-strings,
Mouth to mouth and hand upon hand, her chosen,
    Fairer than all men;

Only saw the beautiful lips and fingers,
Full of songs and kisses and little whispers,
Full of music; only beheld among them
    Soar, as a bird soars

Newly fledged, her visible song, a marvel,
Made of perfect sound and exceeding passion,
Sweetly shapen, terrible, full of thunders,
    Clothed with the wind's wings.

Then rejoiced she, laughing with love, and scattered
Roses, awful roses of holy blossom;
Then the Loves thronged sadly with hidden faces
    Round Aphrodite,

Then the Muses, stricken at heart, were silent;
Yea, the gods waxed pale; such a song was that song.
All reluctant, all with a fresh repulsion,
    Fled from before her.

All withdrew long since, and the land was barren,
Full of fruitless women and music only.
Now perchance, when winds are assuaged at sunset,
    Lull'd at the dewfall,

By the grey sea-side, unassuaged, unheard of,
Unbeloved, unseen in the ebb of twilight,
Ghosts of outcast women return lamenting,
    Purged not in Lethe,

Clothed about with flame and with tears, and singing
Songs that move the heart of the shaken heaven,
Songs that break the heart of the earth with pity,
    Hearing, to hear them.

from *Anactoria*

Ah, take no thought for Love's sake; shall this be,
And she who loves thy lover not love thee?
Sweet soul, sweet mouth of all that laughs and lives,
Mine is she, very mine; and she forgives.
For I beheld in sleep the light that is
In her high place in Paphos, heard the kiss
Of body and soul that mix with eager tears
And laughter stinging through the eyes and ears;
Saw Love, as burning flame from crown to feet,
Imperishable, upon her storied seat;
Clear eyelids lifted toward the north and south,

A mind of many colours, and a mouth
Of many tunes and kisses; and she bowed,
With all her subtle face laughing aloud,
Bowed down upon me, saying, 'Who doth thee wrong,
Sappho?' but thou – thy body is the song,
Thy mouth the music; thou art more than I,
Though my voice die not till the whole world die;
Though men that hear it madden; though love weep,
Though nature change, though shame be charmed to sleep.
Ah, wilt thou slay me lest I kiss thee dead?
Yet the queen laughed from her sweet heart and said:
'Even she that flies shall follow for thy sake,
And she shall give thee gifts that would not take,
Shall kiss that would not kiss thee' (yea, kiss me)
'When thou wouldst not' – when I would not kiss thee!
Ah, more to me than all men as thou art,
Shall not my songs assuage her at the heart?
Ah, sweet to me as life seems sweet to death,
Why should her wrath fill thee with fearful breath?
Nay, sweet, for is she God alone? hath she
Made earth and all the centuries of the sea,
Taught the sun ways to travel, woven most fine
The moonbeams, shed the starbeams forth as wine,
Bound with her myrtles, beaten with her rods,
The young men and the maidens and the gods?
Have we not lips to love with, eyes for tears,
And summer and flower of women and of years?
Stars for the foot of morning, and for noon
Sunlight, and exaltation of the moon;
Waters that answer waters, fields that wear
Lilies, and languor of the Lesbian air?
Beyond those flying feet of fluttered doves,
Are there not other gods for other loves?
Yea, though she scourge thee, sweetest, for my sake,
Blossom not thorns, and flowers not blood should break.
Ah that my lips were tuneless lips, but pressed
To the bruised blossom of thy scourged white breast! ...

MICHAEL FIELD
Katherine Bradley, Edith Cooper

from *Long Ago*

XIV

Τὸ μέλημα τοὖμον·
[My darling]

Atthis, my darling, thou did'st stray
A few feet to the rushy bed,
When a great fear and passion shook
My heart lest haply thou wert dead;
It grew so still about the brook,
As if a soul were drawn away.

Anon thy clear eyes, silver-blue,
Shone through the tamarisk-branches fine;
To pluck me iris thou had'st sprung
Through galingale and celandine;
Away, away the flowers I flung
And thee down to my breast I drew.

My darling! Nay, our very breath
Nor light nor darkness shall divide;
Queen Dawn shall find us on one bed,
Nor must thou flutter from my side
An instant, lest I feel the dread,
Atthis, the immanence of death.

XXX

Πολὺ πακτίδος ἀδυμελεστέρα, χρυσῶ χρυσοτέρα·
[Sweeter far than the harp, more gold than gold]

Thine elder that I am, thou must not cling
To me, nor mournful for my love entreat:

And yet, Alcaeus, as the sudden spring
Is love, yea, and to veiled Demeter sweet.

Sweeter than tone of harp, more gold than gold
Is thy young voice to me; yet, ah, the pain
To learn I am beloved now I am old,
Who, in my youth, loved, as thou must, in vain.

XXXV

Ἀλλά, μὴ μεγαλύνεο δακτυλίῳ πέρι·
[But do not give yourself airs because of a finger-ring]

Come, Gorgo, put the rug in place,
    And passionate recline;
I love to see thee in thy grace,
    Dark, virulent, divine.
But wherefore thus thy proud eyes fix
    Upon a jewelled band?
Art thou so glad the sardonyx
    Becomes thy shapely hand?

Bethink thee! 'Tis for such as thou
    Zeus leaves his lofty seat;
'Tis at thy beauty's bidding how
    Man's mortal life shall fleet;
Those fairest hands – dost thou forget
    Their power to thrill and cling?
O foolish woman, dost thou set
    Thy pride upon a ring?

XLIV

Οὔ τί μοι ὔμμες·
[You are nought to me]

Nought to me! So I choose to say:
We meet, old friends, about the bay;

The golden pulse grows on the shore –
Are not all things as heretofore
Now we have cast our love away?

Men throng us; thou art nought to me,
Therefore, indifferent, I can see
Within thine eyes the bright'ning grace
That once thou gavest face to face;
'Tis natural they welcome thee!

Nought to me, like the silver ring,
Thy mislaid, worthless gift. Last spring,
As any careless girl, I lost
The pin, yet, by the tears it cost,
It should have been worth cherishing.

Nought, nought! and yet if thou dost pass
I grow as summer-coloured grass,
And if I wrap my chiton round,
I know thine ear hath caught the sound,
Although thou heedest not, alas!

Nought to me! Wherefore dost thou throw
On me that glittering glance, as though,
Friend, I had ever done thee wrong,
When the crowd asks me for the song,
'Atthis, I loved thee long ago'?

'Why are women silent? Is it true'

Why are women silent? Is it true,
As he thinks, they are not poets just because they dare not woo?
Let them sing themselves their passions Nature resonant all
    through!

O Christina, by thy cry of pain,
Sappho by thy deadly sweat, I answer women can attain
The great measures of the masters only if they love in vain.

A. E. HOUSMAN

from *Epithalamium*

Happy bridegroom, Hesper brings
All desired and timely things.
All whom morning sends to roam,
Hesper loves to lead them home.
Home return who him behold,
Child to mother, sheep to fold,
Bird to nest from wandering wide:
Happy bridegroom, seek your bride.

from *More Poems*

X

The weeping Pleiads wester,
   And the moon is under seas;
From bourn to bourn of midnight
   Far sighs the rainy breeze:

It sighs from a lost country
   To a land I have not known;
The weeping Pleiads wester,
   And I lie down alone.

XI

The rainy Pleiads wester,
   Orion plunges prone,
The stroke of midnight ceases,
   And I lie down alone.

The rainy Pleiads wester
   And seek beyond the sea
The head that I shall dream of,
   And 'twill not dream of me.

BLISS CARMAN

from *Sappho: One hundred lyrics*

Sappho, who broke off a fragment of her soul for us to guess at

V

O Aphrodite,
God-born and deathless,
Break not my spirit
With bitter anguish:
Thou wilful empress,
I pray thee, hither!

As once aforetime
Well thou didst hearken
To my voice far off, –
Listen, and leaving
Thy father's golden
House in yoked chariot,

Come, thy fleet sparrows
Beating the mid-air
Over the dark earth.
Suddenly near me,
Smiling, immortal,
Thy bright regard asked

What had befallen, –
Why I had called thee, –
What my mad heart then
Most was desiring.
'What fair thing wouldst thou
Lure now to love thee?

'Who wrongs thee, Sappho?
If now she flies thee,
Soon shall she follow; –
Scorning thy gifts now,
Soon be the giver; –
And a loth loved one

'Soon be the lover.'
So even now, too,
Come and release me
From mordant love pain,
And all my heart's will
Help me accomplish!

VI

Peer of the gods he seems,
Who in thy presence
Sits and hears close to him
Thy silver speech-tones
And lovely laughter.

Ah, but the heart flutters
Under my bosom,
When I behold thee
Even a moment;
Utterance leaves me;

My tongue is useless;
A subtle fire
Runs through my body;
My eyes are sightless,
And my ears ringing;

I flush with fever,
And a strong trembling
Lays hold upon me;
Paler than grass am I,
Half dead for madness.

Yet must I, greatly
Daring, adore thee,
As the adventurous
Sailor makes seaward
For the lost sky-line

And undiscovered
Fabulous islands,
Drawn by the lure of
Beauty and summer
And the sea's secret.

      XXI

Softly the first step of twilight
Falls on the darkening dial,
One by one kindle the lights
    In Mitylene.

Noises are hushed in the courtyard,
The busy day is departing,
Children are called from their games, –
    Herds from their grazing.

And from the deep-shadowed angles
Comes the soft murmur of lovers,
Then through the quiet of dusk
    Bright sudden laughter.

From the hushed street, through the portal,
Where soon my lover will enter,
Comes the pure strain of a flute
    Tender with passion.

XXIII

I loved thee, Atthis, in the long ago,
When the great oleanders were in flower
In the broad herded meadows full of sun.
And we would often at the fall of dusk
Wander together by the silver stream,
When the soft grass-heads were all wet with dew,
And purple-misted in the fading light.
And joy I knew and sorrow at thy voice,
And the superb magnificence of love, –
The loneliness that saddens solitude,
And the sweet speech that makes it durable, –
The bitter longing and the keen desire,
The sweet companionship through quiet days
In the slow ample beauty of the world,
And the unutterable glad release
Within the temple of the holy night.
O Atthis, how I loved thee long ago
In that fair perished summer by the sea!

XLII

O heart of insatiable longing,
What spell, what enchantment allures thee
Over the rim of the world
With the sails of the sea-going ships?

And when the rose-petals are scattered
At dead of still noon on the grass-plot,
What means this passionate grief, –
This infinite ache of regret?

LXIII

A beautiful child is mine,
Formed like a golden flower
Cleis the loved one.
And above her I value
Not all the Lydian land
Nor lovely Hellas.

EDWIN ARLINGTON ROBINSON

Doricha

So now the very bones of you are gone
Where they were dust and ashes long ago;
And there was the last ribbon you tied on
To bind your hair, and that is dust also;
And somewhere there is dust that was of old
A soft and scented garment that you wore –
The same that once till dawn did closely fold
You in with fair Charaxus, fair no more.

But Sappho, and the white leaves of her song,
Will make your name a word for all to learn,
And all to love thereafter, even while
It's but a name; and this will be as long
As there are distant ships that will return
Again to Naucratis and to the Nile.

from the Greek of Posidippus

AMY LOWELL

from *The Sisters*

Taking us by and large, we're a queer lot
We women who write poetry. And when you think
How few of us there've been, it's queerer still.
I wonder what it is that makes us do it,
Singles us out to scribble down, man-wise,
The fragments of ourselves. Why are we
Already mother-creatures, double-bearing,
With matrices in body and in brain?
I rather think that there is just the reason
We are so sparse a kind of human being;
The strength of forty thousand Atlases
Is needed for our every-day concerns.
There's Sapho, now I wonder what was Sapho.
I know a single slender thing about her:
That, loving, she was like a burning birch-tree
All tall and glittering fire, and that she wrote
Like the same fire caught up to Heaven and held there,
A frozen blaze before it broke and fell.
Ah, me! I wish I could have talked to Sapho,
Surprised her reticences by flinging mine
Into the wind. This tossing off of garments
Which cloud the soul is none too easy doing
With us to-day. But still I think with Sapho
One might accomplish it, were she in the mood
To bare her loveliness of words and tell
The reasons, as she possibly conceived them,
Of why they are so lovely. Just to know
How she came at them, just to watch
The crisp sea sunshine playing on her hair,
And listen, thinking all the while 'twas she
Who spoke and that we two were sisters
Of a strange, isolated little family.
And she is Sapho – Sapho – not Miss or Mrs.,
A leaping fire we call so for convenience;
But Mrs. Browning – who would ever think

Of such presumption as to call her 'Ba.'
Which draws the perfect line between sea-cliffs
And a close-shuttered room in Wimpole Street.
Sapho could fly her impulses like bright
Balloons tip-tilting to a morning air
And write about it. Mrs. Browning's heart
Was squeezed in stiff conventions. So she lay
Stretched out upon a sofa, reading Greek
And speculating, as I must suppose,
In just this way on Sapho; all the need,
The huge, imperious need of loving, crushed
Within the body she believed so sick.
And it was sick, poor lady, because words
Are merely simulacra after deeds
Have wrought a pattern; when they take the place
Of actions they breed a poisonous miasma
Which, though it leave the brain, eats up the body.
So Mrs. Browning, aloof and delicate,
Lay still upon her sofa, all her strength
Going to uphold her over-topping brain.
It seems miraculous, but she escaped
To freedom and another motherhood
Than that of poems. She was a very woman
And needed both.

SARA TEASDALE

To Cleïs

(The daughter of Sappho)

When the dusk was wet with dew,
    Cleïs, did the muses nine
    Listen in a silent line
While your mother sang to you?

Did they weep or did they smile
    When she crooned to still your cries,
    She, a muse in human guise,
Who forsook her lyre awhile?

Did you feel her wild heart beat?
    Did the warmth of all the sun
    Through your little body run
When she kissed your hands and feet?

Did your fingers, babywise,
    Touch her face and touch her hair,
    Did you think your mother fair,
Could you bear her burning eyes?

Are the songs that soothed your fears
    Vanished like a vanished flame,
    Save the line where shines your name
Starlike down the graying years? …

Cleïs speaks no word to me,
    For the land where she has gone
    Lies as still at dusk and dawn
As a windless, tideless sea.

from *Sappho*

I

Midnight, and in the darkness not a sound,
So, with hushed breathing, sleeps the autumn night;
Only the white immortal stars shall know,
Here in the house with the low-lintelled door,
How, for the last time, I have lit the lamp.
I think you are not wholly careless now,
Walls that have sheltered me so many an hour,
Bed that has brought me ecstasy and sleep,
Floors that have borne me when a gale of joy
Lifted my soul and made me half a god.
Farewell! Across the threshold many feet
Shall pass, but never Sappho's feet again.
Girls shall come in whom love has made aware
Of all their swaying beauty – they shall sing,
But never Sappho's voice, like golden fire,
Shall seek for heaven thru your echoing rafters.
There shall be swallows bringing back the spring
Over the long blue meadows of the sea,
And south-wind playing on the reeds of rain,
But never Sappho's whisper in the night,
Never her love-cry when the lover comes.
Farewell! I close the door and make it fast.

     *   *   *   *   *   *

The little street lies meek beneath the moon,
Running, as rivers run, to meet the sea.
I too go seaward and shall not return.
Oh garlands on the doorposts that I pass,
Woven of asters and of autumn leaves,
I make a prayer for you: Cypris be kind,
That every lover may be given love.
I shall not hasten lest the paving stones
Should echo with my sandals and awake
Those who are warm beneath the cloak of sleep,
Lest they should rise and see me and should say,
'Whither goes Sappho lonely in the night?'

Whither goes Sappho? Whither all men go,
But they go driven, straining back with fear,
And Sappho goes as lightly as a leaf
Blown from brown autumn forests to the sea.

*   *   *   *   *   *

Here on the rock Zeus lifted from the waves,
I shall await the waking of the dawn,
Lying beneath the weight of dark as one
Lies breathless, till the lover shall awake.
And with the sun the sea shall cover me –
I shall be less than the dissolving foam
Murmuring and melting on the ebbing tide;
I shall be less than spindrift, less than shells;
And yet I shall be greater than the gods,
For destiny no more can bow my soul
As rain bows down the watch-fires on the hills.
Yea, if my soul escape it shall aspire
To the white heaven as flame that has its will.
I go not bitterly, not dumb with pain,
Not broken by the ache of love – I go
As one grown tired lies down and hopes to sleep.
Yet they shall say: 'It was for Cercolas;
She died because she could not bear her love.'
They shall remember how we used to walk
Here on the cliff beneath the oleanders
In the long limpid twilight of the spring,
Looking toward Lemnos, where the amber sky
Was pierced with the faint arrow of a star.
How should they know the wind of a new beauty
Sweeping my soul had winnowed it with song?
I have been glad tho' love should come or go,
Happy as trees that find a wind to sway them,
Happy again when it has left them rest.
Others shall say, 'Grave Dica wrought her death
She would not lift her lips to take a kiss,
Or ever lift her eyes to take a smile.
She was a pool the winter paves with ice
That the wild hunter in the hills must leave

With thirst unslaked in the brief southward sun.'
Ah Dica, it is not for thee I go;
And not for Phaon, tho' his ship lifts sail
Here in the windless harbor for the south.
Oh, darkling deities that guard the Nile,
Watch over one whose gods are far away.
Egypt, be kind to him, his eyes are deep –
Yet they are wrong who say it was for him.
How should they know that Sappho lived and died
Faithful to love, not faithful to the lover,
Never transfused and lost in what she loved,
Never so wholly loving nor at peace.
I asked for something greater than I found,
And every time that love has made me weep,
I have rejoiced that love could be so strong;
For I have stood apart and watched my soul
Caught in the gust of passion, as a bird
With baffled wings against the dusty whirlwind
Struggles and frees itself to find the sky.
It is not for a single god I go;
I have grown weary of the winds of heaven.
I will not be a reed to hold the sound
Of whatsoever breath the gods may blow,
Turning my torment into music for them.
They gave me life; the gift was bountiful,
I lived with the swift singing strength of fire,
Seeking for beauty as a flame for fuel –
Beauty in all things and in every hour.
The gods have given life – I gave them song;
The debt is paid and now I turn to go.

      ★   ★   ★   ★   ★   ★

The breath of dawn blows the stars out like lamps,
There is a rim of silver on the sea,
As one grown tired who hopes to sleep, I go.

EZRA POUND

Ιμέρρω

Thy soul
Grown delicate with satieties,
Atthis.
O Atthis,
I long for thy lips.
I long for thy narrow breasts,
Thou restless, ungathered.

Ιμέρρω, I desire

EDNA ST VINCENT MILLAY

Sappho Crosses the Dark River into Hades

Charon, indeed, your dreaded oar,
With what a peaceful sound it dips
Into the stream; how gently, too,
From the wet blade the water drips.

I knew a ferryman before.
But he was not so old as you.
He spoke from unembittered lips,
With careless eyes on the bright sea
One day, such bitter words to me
As age and wisdom never knew.

This was a man of meagre fame;
He ferried merchants from the shore
To Mitylene (whence I came)
On Lesbos; Phaon is his name.

I hope that he will never die,
As I have done, and come to dwell
In this pale city we approach.
Not that, indeed, I wish him well,
(Though never have I wished him harm)
But rather that I hope to find
In some unechoing street of Hell
The peace I long have had in mind:
A peace whereon may not encroach
That supple back, the strong brown arm,
That curving mouth, the sunburned curls;
But rather that I would rely,
Having come so far, at such expense,
Upon some quiet lodging whence
I need not hear his voice go by
In scraps of talk with boys and girls.

CAROLYN KIZER

from *For Sappho/After Sappho*

I
and you sang eloquently
for my pleasure
before I knew
you were girl or boy

    at the moment
    dawn awoke me
    you were in my bed

not sister not lover
fierce though you were
a small cat
with thorny claws

    any daughter
    seeking comfort

you asked what you could give
to one who you thought
possessed everything

    then you forgot giving
    and tried to take
    blindly seeking the breast

what to do but hold you
lost innocent...

    we love whatever
    caresses us
    in need or pleasure
    a debt a favor
    a desperation

you were already
a speaking instrument
I loved the speaker
loved the voice
as it broke my heart with pity

    breath immortal
    the words nothing
    articulate poems
    not pertinent   the breath
    everything

you the green shoot
I the ripe earth
not yours to possess
alas not yours

JOHN HOLLANDER

After an Old Text

His head is in the heavens, who across the
Narrow canyon of pillow from yours harkens
With gazing hand and hearing knees through darkness,
    Looking and listening

To the sweet quietude of terminating
Conversation, the gentle brief wake for the
Long-dead day, the keening of his shortened
    Breath on your shoulder:

This revision of you sucks out the sound of
Words from my mouth, my tongue collapses, my legs
Flag, my ears roar, my eyes are blind with flame; my
    Head is in hell then.

Cleis

She was young. The jeep was yellow. She
cruised past; her style was studied – a white
shirt crisply collared: a visitation, or
an extrapolation, from Sappho's
grove. Invitations had prevented our day
in bed, and we were suffering. Flowers, sun –

we had left brunch. A young woman in a sun
chariot, eyes burning beneath blond bangs, she
drove slowly toward us, a clean car. 'Good day,'
she said. You noted the greeting. The white
pelargonium were still in bloom. Sappho's
girls would be weaving them into garlands, or

dancing, singing what the scent inspired, or
quilling lyres. She leaned out the window, sun
glinting off her tousled brow. Sappho
would have applauded her approach, how she
directed her gaze without guile, whites
of her eyes cossetting blue irises. 'Good day'

was perhaps not all she said. It was Sunday
in California, weather like paradise or
Lesbos, clouds seductively adrift, white
as if to reassert cloud, reflecting sun-
light. Our music had begun, our swoon, when she
drove down the hill and hovered. Was she Sappho's

gold-dressed daughter Cleis? Or Sappho's
dapple-throned Aphrodite, girl for a day,
oaring down from heaven in a gold car? She
slowed nonetheless, as if she expected us, or
had perhaps conjured us. We wore sun-
glasses, so she was not an attack of white

blindness, or any blindness. She was a white-
kirtled vision to tease us back to Sappho's –
dare I speak it? – bower; a trenchant, sun-
drenched mirage to accentuate a day
we were taken transcendentally, or
at least fervently, with one another. She

accelerated. White wheels whirled into day,
and, as Sappho's jeep, emblazoned NO NUKES OR
WIFE ABUSE flashed in the sun and vanished, so did she.

MICHAEL LONGLEY

The Evening Star

in memory of Catherine Mercer, 1994–1996

The day we buried your two years and two months
So many crocuses and snowdrops came out for you
I tried to isolate from those galaxies one flower:
A snowdrop appeared in the sky at dayligone,

The evening star, the star in Sappho's epigram
Which brings back everything that shiny daybreak
Scatters, which brings the sheep and brings the goat
And brings the wean back home to her mammy.

dayligone, twilight

OLGA BROUMAS and JANE MILLER

Third Epitaph

Under the black leaves of the laurels, the amorous
flowers of the rose, here I have lain who knew to comb
verse on verse and make a kiss flower.

I grew up in the land of nymphs; I lived on the island
of women friends; I died on the Cyprian island. This is
why my name is illustrious and my column anointed with oil.

Do not cry, you who stop: I was given a beautiful
funeral; the female mourners tore their cheeks; they put
my mirrors and necklaces in my tomb.

And now, on the pale prairies of asphodel, I promenade,
impalpable shadow, and the memory of my terrestrial life
is my subterranean joy.

from PIERRE LOUŸS: *Chansons de Bilitis*

Index to Sappho's Poems

References to Sappho's poems and fragments are given on the left according to the now standard numbering of Edgar Lobel and Denys Page in *Poetarum Lesbiorum Fragmenta* (1955). Not listed is the epigraph to poem XLIV on p. 121, which is no. 43 in E. Diehl, *Anthologia Lyrica* (1922–5). On the right are page numbers for the versions of and references to Sappho's poems and fragments as they appear in this book.